WHITE GRASS

GRASS

flavor

Laurie Little
Mary Beth Gwyer

with Mary Anders and Amy Bonfiglio

International Standard Book Number

ISBN – 10   159975-015-5
ISBN – 13   978-1-59975-015-6

Library of Congress Cataloging-in-Publication Data
Printed in the United States of America
Copyright © 2005 by White Grass Ski Touring Center

White Grass Ski Touring Center
HC 70 Box 299
Davis, WV 26260
304-866-4114
www.whitegrass.com
(email) chip@whitegrass.com

1st Printing – 2005
2nd Printing – 2007

Master Craft Printers
100 East Liberty St.
Oakland, MD 21550 – 1202

2007

For our Mothers,
Jeanette and Gerry

Who, through their

wisdom and patience,

gave us a true

appreciation of good food.

And a special thanks to White Grass,
especially Chip Chase and Randall Reed
for letting us do what we love
for the last twenty-five years.

A wise person once told me that food is how we mother ourselves. Sure it's about nutrition, but mostly it's about feeling good. It brings pleasure and comfort, it heals our wounds and makes us whole again.

Here in Canaan, food brings us together like nothing else. We cook to connect with friends and to show off a little. When you exercise in this beautiful playground, as we do, you get hungry. And you don't feel so guilty about eating heartily.

But The folks who work and play at White Grass are the best cooks of all. They love good food, but they're practical, too. They live close to nature and use natural ingredients. They know that vegetables must taste good if you want people to eat them. They know what to substitute when a fancy ingredient is missing at the store. They know how to cook for a crowd, clean up quickly and still feel like skiing when it's over.

You can learn a lot about cooking from folks who use fresh ingredients and make their food from scratch. But what you can't learn is the love that goes into every dish they cook. It's that love—a mother's love—that Laurie and Mary Beth offer you in this book.

So eat up—it's good for you.

Susan Moore, *Bright Morning Inn,* Davis, West Virginia

Forward

For nearly a quarter of a century, **White Grass Ski Touring and Cafe** has welcomed cross country skiers. Our lodge, located in Canaan Valley, West Virginia, was home of the Weiss Knob Ski Area in the late 1950's. Here lies some of the most beautiful and varied mountain terrain in the East. With an average snowfall of 150 inches, there is no shortage of winter fun.

In all this time, the **White Grass Cafe** has served thousands of hungry visitors offering daily lunches and weekend dinners during ski season. The setting is unassuming and homey; we offer "not your average fare, in not your average restaurant."

When we wrote our first cookbook in 1996, we just wanted to share our favorite recipes with friends and families. We had no idea that our book would be so welcomed by so many. It sparked us to think more about what we eat and how it affects our health.

Fresh, natural, flavorful and creative are the words that best describe the intentions of our culinary creations. We have worked hard to do more than just make food. We have strived to maintain interesting tastes and flavors. There's nothing like a hot bowl of homemade, silky *Wild Rice and Mushroom* or savory *Asian Chicken Noodle Soup* after an exhilarating romp in the snow. We hasten to add that you don't have to be a skier to enjoy our recipes.

With *Flavor*, we have collected a variety of recipes that we hope will thrill your taste buds, satisfy your hunger and feed your soul. We have continued in the style of *Cross Country Cooking* emphasizing ease of preparation, flavor diversity and simplicity. This book is a gathering of ideas; of things we have done and places we have been in the last few years. Loves and likes, people and activities, beliefs and consequences are what make us and are reflected through our cooking. We hope this book will inspire new experiences even if only to offer a new taste your palate has never experienced before.

Unconditional or unrestricted is the best way to describe the way we cook. We try to maintain a relaxed cooking style with a loose guideline of "eat what's good when it's good." By starting with foods in their natural state, we make the best of them using a little instinct and a little creativity. When it comes to food, recipes and trends come and go. Taste is one thing that doesn't change—the taste of good food.

Keeping it simple encourages you to experiment with ingredients and techniques. We have offered suggestions throughout the book. We don't mean to be ambiguous, just to stimulate creativity. Not that there is anything wrong with being precise. When baking, especially, measurements need to be exact. But ingredients can vary.

It has been a joy and an honor to be able to work together and with our friends to create this compilation. We are so grateful to be living amongst enlightened, active, life-loving people who inspire us and remind us that education is continual and *carpe diem* is a way of life. We hope you enjoy **White Grass Flavor** and that our recipes spark your own culinary creativity.

Laurie Little and Mary Beth Gwyer

> *When it comes to food, recipes and trends come and go. Taste is one thing that doesn't change— the taste of good food.*

Table of Contents

Appetizers

Hot Artichoke and Spinach Dip

Cheese Fondue

Veggie Pot Stickers

Mini Spicy Crab Cakes

Lettuce Wraps

Curried Cheese Ball

White Grass Bruschetta

Spicy Shrimp Spread

Quiche Squares

Stuffed Grape Leaves

Layered Mediterranean Dip

Thai Eggplant Dip

West Virginia Sushi Rolls

Italian Sausage Stuffed Mushrooms

Hot Artichoke & Spinach Dip

This recipe could be Chip's Cousin Lila's claim to fame. It's far from low fat, but it's always the hit at the Café!

Preheat oven to 350°F.

Soften cream cheese at room temperature or put into microwave on defrost cycle for 30 seconds or until soft.

In a bowl, mix cream cheese, sour cream, mayonnaise, artichokes, garlic, cheese and hot pepper in a bowl and mix well.

Squeeze liquid from spinach then add to the dip mixture. Stir to combine.

Place dip into a shallow baking dish and bake for 25 to 30 minutes or until the edges start to brown. Serve with good crusty bread pieces or whole grain crackers.

This can be made ahead of time and baked just before serving.

Serves 6.

8   oz. cream cheese

⅓   cup sour cream

⅓   cup mayonnaise

1   (16 oz.) can artichoke hearts, drained and quartered

2   cloves garlic, minced

1   Tbs. chopped jalapeño pepper

⅔   cup Parmesan or Pecorino Romano cheese, grated

1   package frozen chopped spinach, thawed

Cheese Fondue

We clear off the coffee table for this appetizer or dinner and gather everyone around to dive into the fondue. The kids love it.

1	clove garlic
12 oz.	cheddar cheese
4 oz.	Gruyere cheese
1 tsp.	cornstarch
1	cup white wine

Cut garlic clove in half and rub the inside of a heavy saucepan with the cut edge of the garlic.

Grate both cheeses into a bowl. Sprinkle with cornstarch and mix.

Heat wine in the saucepan to a slight boil and slowly add cheeses, stirring frequently until smooth.

Keep warm or place in a fondue pot and serve as a dip with crusty ciabatta or French bread.

Other dipping options:

sliced tart apples • sliced pears • grapes
lightly steamed broccoli • asparagus • cauliflower
steamed small red potatoes (firm) • grape tomatoes
steamed shrimp

Tip: Stir the fondue with a back and forth motion instead of a circular motion to keep the cheese from becoming rubbery.

Veggie Pot Stickers

To be honest, this is a project dish. It is really more time consuming than technically difficult but, is totally worth it. Get a buddy to help fill the dumplings. It can be fun.

Heat a large skillet or wok over medium-high heat. Add oil then add veggies, one at a time. Begin with cabbage then onions, garlic, pepper, carrots, mushrooms and spinach, in that order, cooking for a minute or two for each addition. Remove from heat, cool slightly and add ginger, soy sauce and sesame oil, mix well.

Fill each wrapper with a heaping tablespoon of filling. Wet your finger and run it around the edge to moisten. Fold in half and gently press out air while pressing edges together with thumb and forefinger to seal. Place on a baking sheet lined with a clean dish towel to prevent from sticking. Fill all dumplings.

To cook, heat a non-stick skillet over medium heat and add a drop of vegetable oil. Place 5 or 6 dumplings in the pan and brown on both sides. Pour in ¼ cup water, cover with a lid and let steam, 2 to 3 minutes. Remove to a large serving plate and continue to cook all dumplings. Serve warm with dipping sauce.

For sauce, mix all ingredients. Serve in a small bowl.

Makes 50 dumplings.

Filling:

- 2 Tbs. vegetable oil
- 3 cups cabbage, shredded
- 1 medium onion, chopped
- 3 cloves garlic, minced
- ½ bell pepper, chopped
- 1 cup carrots, shredded
- 1 cup mushrooms, chopped
- ½ pound fresh spinach
- 1 Tbs. fresh ginger, grated
- 1 Tbs. soy sauce
- 1 tsp. sesame oil
- 1 pkg. round wonton wrappers

Dipping Sauce

- ½ cup soy sauce
- 1 Tbs. fresh ginger, grated
- 1 tsp. sesame oil
- ½ tsp. crushed red pepper
- ¼ tsp. sugar

Mini Spicy Crab Cakes

Jump start your taste buds with this fired-up version of our original crab cake recipe. On an hors d'oeuvre buffet, these always go first.

1	egg, beaten
2	Tbs. mayonnaise
1	Tbs. Dijon mustard
1	tsp. Worcestershire sauce
2	tsp. Old Bay seasoning
1	tsp. lemon juice
1½	tsp. hot sauce
1	pound crabmeat
¾	cup breadcrumbs
	Peanut oil for cooking

Combine first seven ingredients in a large bowl. Mix thoroughly. Gently fold in crabmeat and breadcrumbs.

Form into 1-inch balls. Heat a skillet, add ¼ cup peanut oil. Place balls into skillet and flatten as they cook, browning on each side.

Serve warm with a dipping sauce, see page 111.

Makes 24 cakes.

Lettuce Wraps

This recipe, from former Café diva, Nancy Mammarella, is a light, clean and refreshing snack. Sometimes she replaces rice paper for the lettuce.

- 1 head bibb or butterhead lettuce
- 1 ripe tomato, sliced, then halved
- 1 bunch fresh basil
- 1 red bell pepper, sliced into strips
- 1 cup mung bean sprouts
- 1 carrot, sliced into strips
- Fresh scallions, cleaned

Wash, dry and separate lettuce leaves. Stuff full of vegetables and roll up.
Serve with cooled dipping sauce.

Other filling options:

- Cooked, peeled shrimp
- Fresh young spinach leaves
- Celery hearts
- Arugula or watercress
- Steamed asparagus
- Cucumber strips
- Fresh snow peas

Peanut Dipping Sauce:

- 2 tsp. vegetable oil
- 1 tsp. fresh chili paste (sambal oelek) or 3 cloves garlic and 1 hot chili, minced
- $\frac{1}{4}$ cup soy sauce
- $\frac{1}{3}$ cup peanut butter
- 1 tsp. sugar
- 1 tsp. fresh grated ginger

In a small saucepan, heat oil over medium heat, add chili paste, stir. Then add 1 cup water, soy sauce, peanut butter, sugar and ginger; cook until thick.

Curried Cheese Ball

Joanne Patterson brought this to our annual Jack Frost celebration. It was a huge hit.

6 oz. cream cheese
1 cup cheddar cheese, grated
1/4 tsp. curry powder
1/2 tsp. garlic powder
4 tsp. sherry
1/2 cup Major Grey's chutney
2 Tbs. green onion, chopped
2 Tbs. peanuts, chopped
4 Tbs. bacon, cooked and crumbled
4 Tbs. coconut, toasted

Mix cream cheese, cheddar, curry, garlic and sherry.

Line a bowl with plastic wrap and pack cheese mixture into it; chill overnight.

Turn ball into a serving dish and remove plastic wrap. Pour chutney over cheese ball.

Sprinkle with green onions, peanuts, bacon and coconut, in that order.

Serves 6 with crackers.

To **toast coconut**, spread evenly on a baking pan. Bake at 300°F until browned, about 20 minutes, stirring occasionally.

White Grass Bruschetta

1 **loaf ciabatta bread (or any crusty Italian loaf)**
Olive oil

Slice bread in ½-inch slices; then cut into bite sized pieces about 2 to 3 inches across. Brush both sides of bread with olive oil. Place on an ungreased cookie sheet and bake at 425°F for 5 minutes, or until lightly browned on both sides. Cool and store in a zip lock bag for up to 24 hours at room temperature.

Olive Tapenade: Blend all in a food processor until smooth.
(Can be made the day before and refrigerated until needed.)

1 **cup Calamata olives, pitted**
1 **tsp. balsamic vinegar**
1 **tsp. olive oil**
2 **tsp. minced garlic**

Tomato Mixture: Mix all ingredients together in a bowl. Best if used right away.

2 **medium ripe red tomatoes, chopped**
1 **ripe yellow tomato, chopped**
⅓ **cup sweet onion, finely chopped**
½ **cup red bell pepper, finely chopped**
½ **cup green bell pepper, finely chopped**
½ **cup yellow bell pepper, finely chopped**
1 **Tbs. olive oil**
1 **Tbs. fresh basil, chopped**
⅛ **tsp. black pepper**
  Parmesan cheese

To serve cold: Just before serving, spread each toast with about one teaspoon of ***Olive Tapenade*** and a spoonful of tomato mixture.

To serve warm: Spread toasts with Tapenade and top with the tomato mixture, then sprinkle with Parmesan and heat at 425°F until cheese melts.

Serves 8 to 10.

Spicy Shrimp Spread

There's nothing like a great make-ahead treat that you can pull out of the fridge for a quick delicious appetizer.

2	cloves garlic
¼	cup onion
¼	cup fresh parsley
2	(8 oz.) cream cheese, room temperature
I	Tbs. lemon juice
I	Tbs. red wine vinegar
I	Tbs. tomato paste
½	tsp. black pepper
¼	tsp. cayenne pepper
¼	tsp. celery seed
½	pound small, cooked shrimp

Using a food processor, finely chop garlic, onions and parsley.

Cut cream cheese into quarters and add, one at a time, until blended with veggies.

Add lemon juice, vinegar, paste and spices and pulse until blended.

Remove from food processor and blend in shrimp.

Serve with sliced vegetables and crackers. This will keep in the fridge for about five days.

If you don't have a food processor, finely mince vegetables and blend all ingredients very well using a large bowl and a wooden spoon.

Larger sized shrimp can also be used, just chop them into smaller pieces.

Serves 12.

Quiche Squares

Here's another versatile recipe. This can be made in two round pie pans and cut into thin wedges or a rectangular pan and cut into squares. Any way it's cut – it tastes great and the flavor options are endless. Feed a crowd with this recipe.

Preheat oven to 350°F.

In a large skillet, over medium-high heat, sauté onions for 3 minutes in oil or until browned. Add peppers and broccoli and sauté about 2 minutes.

Spread cooked veggies over 9×13-inch pan and cover with cheese. Arrange sliced tomatoes over cheese.

In a separate bowl, whisk eggs and milk. Add flour, baking powder and seasonings and beat until smooth. Pour over vegetables.

Bake for 45 to 55 minutes or until set and browned. Cool and cut into 1½-inch squares.

Serves 10 to 15.

Optional ingredients:

sautéed, sliced mushrooms
asparagus • fresh spinach • feta cheese • Parmesan
fresh basil • diced ham • smoked gouda • artichoke hearts

1	Tbs. olive oil
1	cup onion, chopped
1	cup red bell peppers, chopped
3	cups broccoli, chopped
1	pint cherry tomatoes, sliced in half
1	cup cheddar cheese, shredded
1	cup jack cheese, shredded
6	large eggs
3	cups milk
1½	cups all-purpose flour
1	tsp. baking powder
1	tsp. salt
½	tsp. black pepper
1	tsp. dried basil

Stuffed Grape Leaves
with Meat in Egg-Lemon Sauce (Dolmas)

"Dolmathes me Kreas Avogolemono"   *George Mikedes*

Dolmathes, also called dolmas, describes little rolls made from leaves stuffed with rice or meat and steamed until cooked.

1   (1 lb.) jar grape leaves (If fresh leaves are available, use the young tender ones)

1½ pounds ground beef (or a mixture of lamb & beef)

½ cup chopped onions

½ cup long grain rice (uncooked)

6   scallions (green onions) chopped

¼ cup pine nuts (optional)

¼ cup chopped fresh mint (optional)

⅓ cup chopped fresh dill

2   Tbs. chopped parsley

2   Tbs. olive oil

Salt & pepper to taste

1   tsp. olive oil to coat pot

Lemon Egg Sauce (following)

Remove the grape leaves from the jar, leaving the brine. Soak or wash leaves thoroughly; drain and separate carefully. With a sharp knife or scissors, cut the heavy stems from the leaves. (If using fresh grape leaves, parboil for 5 minutes, then drain.)

Mix ground meat, chopped onions, rice, scallions, pine nuts, dill, mint, parsley, olive oil, salt and pepper. Oil a heavy pot, line with a few grape leaves, set aside.

To stuff a grape leaf: place on working surface rough side up, stem toward you. Place a tablespoon full of the meat/rice mixture near the stem end. Fold the bottom of the leaf nearest you up and over the filling, then the right side over the filling, next the left side and roll tightly toward the pointed end of the leaf. Place the dolma, seam side down, in the pot. Continue stuffing/rolling grape leaves until the mixture has been used, always placing the seam side down. Dolmas can be stacked up in layers, just make sure you weigh them down so they don't unroll while cooking. Place a heavy, inverted plate over the dolmas. Add enough water to cover the dolmas, about 2 cups. Bring to a boil, cover pot, reduce to simmer for 50 minutes or until rice is cooked, adding more water as necessary to cover plate. Shake pan gently while cooking to prevent sticking. When rice is done, remove from heat, but keep hot while preparing egg-lemon sauce. (Pour off the broth to use for the following recipe, leaving dolmas in the pot.)

Egg Lemon Sauce

"The secret of this delicate sauce, the great grandfather of the hollandaise sauce, is mixing the eggs and lemon juice with the hot broth slowly, to avoid curdling and cooking the egg. My grandmother, while slowly and carefully adding the broth to the egg-lemon mixture, would make a kissing sound over the pot, a 'magical' technique to 'sweeten and appease the fates', to keep the eggs from curdling, the sauce from spoiling. Today we know to keep the temperature below 160° to keep the sauce from curdling."

George Mikedes

3 eggs, separated

Juice of 2 large lemons, strained

Hot broth from the dolma pot

Beat yolks well in a medium sized bowl. In a separate bowl whip egg whites until stiff & peaked. Gradually add yolks and lemon juice while continuing to beat. Slowly add the hot, but not boiling, broth from the pot. Do not let the eggs curdle by adding the hot broth too quickly. (Boiling broth or stock will cook the eggs & ruin the dish.) Pour the entire egg mixture into the dolmas pot. Gently shake the pot to distribute the mixture throughout the broth, creating the egg-lemon sauce.

Serve with crusty bread and Salata Horiatiko; a country Greek salad: Sliced, peeled and seeded cucumber, feta cheese, olives, diced fresh tomatoes, thinly sliced red or green onion, with a dressing of oil & vinegar, oregano, salt & pepper to taste.

This dish is much easier to make than it sounds.
Try it—you'll love it.

"Kalee Orexi"—Good Appetite!

Early Greeks used fig leaves and leaves from the mulberry & hazelnut trees, but legend has it that this recipe was born when Alexander the Great destroyed Thebes. Food was so scarce the Thebans had to finely chop the little meat they had and roll it, with rice, into grape leaves. The dish was refined during the Byzantine era with the optional ingredients mentioned. Farther east, the dish becomes more exotic with the addition of currants, sweet meats and raisins.

Layered Mediterranean Dip

This is a twist on the well known Seven Layer Mexican dip. Make it easy on yourself by using quality store bought hummus. Serve with pita or crusty bread.

8   oz. prepared hummus

8   oz. olive tapenade or chopped calamata olives (see tapenade recipe on page 19)

4   oz. feta cheese

1   cup tomatoes, chopped

¼   cup red onion, chopped

½   cup fresh parsley, chopped

1   cucumber, sliced

Using a small round or square deep glass dish, start by layering bottom with hummus. Continue to layer with tapenade or chopped olives, then crumbled feta, tomatoes and top with a mixture of onion and parsley. Place sliced cucumber around the edge of the dish for garnish.

Vary this hors d'oeuvre by using:

artichoke hearts • pesto • sprouts • goat cheese

roasted red peppers • chopped scallions

chopped peperoncini

Thai Eggplant Dip

This is a favorite of Mary Anders, former Café chef and true vegetarian.

Cut off eggplant stems. Pierce eggplant several times with a fork and place on a baking sheet covered with foil.

Cook in a preheated 350°F oven until very soft; about one hour. Remove to cool. When cool enough to handle, peel skins from eggplant.

With the motor running on a food processor, add garlic and ginger; mince. Add eggplant and process until smooth.

Add remaining ingredients and salt to taste.

Can be refrigerated up to 4 days or frozen.

Serve with warm pita triangles.

Makes about 2½ cups.

2	medium eggplants
4	cloves garlic
1	Tbs. fresh ginger, minced
2	Tbs. soy sauce
2	Tbs. rice vinegar
1	Tbs. sesame oil
1	Tbs. fresh cilantro, minced
½	tsp. red pepper flakes, crushed
	Salt to taste

West Virginia Sushi Rolls

We take advantage of our local foods – smoked trout being one of the best.
Making sushi is not difficult. My friend Lara Harvey taught me how.
Get the obscure ingredients from an Asian market. MBG

2	cups sushi rice
3	cups water
2	Tbs. rice vinegar
2	Tbs. sugar
I	tsp. salt
I	medium cucumber
I	bunch of scallions
I	red or yellow bell pepper
2	carrots
8	oz. cream cheese
4	oz. smoked trout
I	pkg. toasted sushi nori sheets
	Pickled ginger
	Soy sauce
	Wasabi

Bring water and rice to a boil in a 2-quart saucepan. Reduce heat, cover and simmer until all liquid is absorbed, about 15 minutes. Remove from heat and let rice set for about 10 minutes.

Mix vinegar, sugar and salt together in a small bowl and stir until sugar dissolves.

Place rice in a wide, shallow glass bowl. Toss rice gently with vinegar mixture, using a plastic spoon. Cool.

Prepare vegetables. Peel cucumber and slice in half lengthwise, scoop out seeds with a spoon and discard. Cut into long thin strips.

Cut bottoms off scallions; trim greens so onions are about 7 inches long.

Slice pepper into long thin strips, about ¼-inch wide or less.

Peel carrot and cut into long thin strips, about ¼-inch wide or less.

Thoroughly mix cream cheese and trout.

To prepare sushi, take 1 sheet of nori. Spread about ¾ cup of rice over the lower half of the nori. Spread a thin 1-inch wide strip of trout mixture (about 2 Tbs.) lengthwise across the middle of the rice. Lay strips of vegetables, grouped next to each other over the trout.

Roll nori sheet tightly starting at rice end. Dip your finger into water and wet end edge of nori to make it stick.

Continue to make rolls until all rice and/or vegetables are used up. Cut each roll into ¾-inch slices. Serve with sliced pickled ginger, wasabi and soy sauce. Eat as soon as you make it. Fresh sushi is best.

Makes 4 to 5 rolls.

Italian Sausage Stuffed Mushrooms

Impress your favorite people with this appetizer.

Preheat oven to 350°F.

In a large skillet, melt butter and gently sauté mushroom caps, about 10 minutes, turning them until tender. Remove from heat, cool.

Dice mushroom stems in a food processor or chop by hand.

Sauté the stems in 2 Tbs. olive oil with garlic, onion and sausage until browned. Drain off any excess grease. Mix in basil, egg, breadcrumbs, tomato sauce and mozzarella.

Stuff the caps with filling.

Sprinkle with Parmesan cheese if desired.

Bake at 350°F for 10 minutes or until the tops brown. Serve warm.

Serves 4.

1 (12 oz.) pkg. mushrooms, cleaned, stems removed and saved

4   Tbs. butter

2   Tbs. olive oil

2   cloves garlic, minced

1   small onion, minced

½   pound Italian sausage (hot or sweet)

½   tsp. dried basil

1   egg

1   cup seasoned bread crumbs

¼   cup tomato sauce

1   cup shredded mozzarella cheese

Parmesan (optional)

Soups

White Bean and Kale

Sicilian Lentil

Cumin Scented Carrot

Black Bean & Sweet Potato Chili

Asian Chicken Noodle

Chicken Galangal

Grandma's Wild Mushroom

Vegetarian Hot and Sour

Wild Rice and Mushroom

Chicken, Rice & Broccoli

Butternut, Fennel & Leek Puree

Roasted Yellow Pepper Soup with Shrimp

Southwestern Chowder

Morgan's Turkey Noodle

Potato & Leek

White Bean & Kale Soup

Nothing is better for a wet, cold, gray day. Using canned beans makes this soup quicker to prepare.

In a large soup pot, heat olive oil over medium-high heat. Add onions and garlic and cook until soft, about 5 minutes. Add carrots and celery and sauté another 3 minutes.

Add broth, beans, salt and pepper and cook on a low simmer for at least 20 minutes.

Add parsley and kale and continue on low for another 20 minutes. Cooking longer will not hurt this soup and it will be even better the next day.

Garnish with your favorite hot sauce, if desired.

Serves 4.

1	Tbs. olive oil
1	medium onion, finely chopped
3	cloves garlic, minced
2	carrots, peeled and diced
1	cup celery, chopped
5	cups veggie broth (see page 33) or chicken broth
2	(16 oz.) cans white beans, rinsed and drained
1/2	tsp. salt
1/2	tsp. black pepper
1/4	cup fresh parsley, chopped or 1 Tbs. dried
1/2	pound kale or swiss chard, washed and torn into pieces

Sicilian Lentil Soup

Since autumn and winter are usually the time for soups, we list dried herbs for use. If you are lucky enough to have fresh, by all means, add them. Increase the measurements when using fresh and adjust to your taste.

2	Tbs. olive oil
1	large onion, diced (about two cups)
3–4	cloves garlic, minced
2	Tbs. dried parsley or $\frac{1}{2}$ cup fresh, chopped
2	cups dried lentils
8	cups water or broth, see page 33
1	(6 oz.) can tomato paste
1	(28 oz.) can diced tomatoes
2	tsp. dried oregano
2	tsp. dried basil
1	tsp. salt
1	tsp. black pepper
$\frac{1}{2}$	tsp. red pepper flakes (optional)

Heat a large soup pot over medium heat. Add oil, wait a minute then add onion and garlic. Sauté until lightly brown, about 4 minutes.

Add parsley, lentils, broth, paste, tomatoes and spices.

Bring to a low boil then simmer on low 45 minutes until lentils are soft.

Serves 4 to 6.

An excellent accompaniment for this or any soup is bread. Try ciabatta or other hearty European style bread. Toast it lightly or grill 1 minute on each side. Take 1 cut clove of garlic and rub it across the bread. Drizzle with olive oil. Enjoy with your soup.

Cumin Scented Carrot Soup

This light, brothy soup has a very unique flavor.

In a soup pot, melt butter over medium heat.

Sauté onions and carrots with sugar, cumin seed and garlic for 5 to 10 minutes.

Pour in wine and continue cooking to reduce the broth by half the amount. Add tomato, stock, and herbs.

Cook until carrots are tender and adjust the salt and seasonings.

Serves 4.

*See page 44 for information on Herbes de Provence.

Making Stock:

Having good stock will make a better soup. Boil pieces, peels and stems (about ⅓ cup each) of onions, carrots, celery, parsley and potatoes in 7 cups of water. Add 1 tsp. salt. Simmer, covered, a minimum of 30 minutes. Strain and use immediately or refrigerate for later use.

If short on time, use bouillon (one cube per two cups of liquid) or vegetable broth powder (2 tsp. per two cups of liquid).

1	Tbs. butter
1	medium onion, chopped
3	carrots, diced
	Pinch of sugar
¼	tsp. cumin seed
5	cloves of garlic, sliced
¾	cup white wine
1	cup tomato, diced, fresh or canned
4	cups vegetable stock
	Pinch of thyme or herbes de provence*
	Salt and pepper to taste

Black Bean & Sweet Potato Chili

This soup can be made relatively quickly and also serves well as a side dish with rice. Of course, like most bean dishes, it tastes even better the next day.

2	medium sweet potatoes
1	Tbs. vegetable oil
1	medium onion, chopped
3	cloves garlic, minced
1	(28 oz.) large can diced tomatoes
3	(15 oz.) cans black beans, rinsed and drained
1	tsp. chili powder
1½	tsp. cumin
1	tsp. salt
½	tsp. black pepper
¾	cup chopped cilantro leaves
2–3	canned chipotle peppers, seeded and chopped

Preheat oven to 375°F and bake sweet potatoes for 45 minutes until cooked through but still firm. Cool.

In a large soup pot, heat oil, then add onions and garlic. Sauté 3 to 4 minutes or until lightly browned. Then add beans, tomatoes and spices, mix. Simmer on low for 20 minutes.

Peel potatoes and cut into ½-inch cubes. Add to beans with 1 cup water.

Add cilantro and peppers and more water, if desired. Continue to cook on low until serving.

Serve 4 as a meal, 8 as a side dish.

Chipotle peppers are smoked jalapenos that are sold canned in adobo (tomato) sauce. They can be purchased in the Hispanic section of most groceries.

Asian Chicken Noodle Soup

This soup has everything—especially lots of flavor.

Chop all vegetables, keep separate.

Heat a large soup pot over medium-high heat. Add oil.

Cook onions 2 minutes then add cabbage. Cook additional 3 minutes, stirring occasionally.

Then add celery, carrots, garlic and peppers, cook 5 minutes.

Add water, salt and chicken parts. Bring to a boil. Simmer 30 minutes on low.

Remove chicken pieces with a slotted spoon, cool. Separate meat from bones and tear into bite-sized pieces; return to soup.

Add greens to broth. Then season soup with soy sauce, ginger and sesame oil. Remove meat from chicken bones and add it to pot. Stir in noodles and simmer until they are cooked, about 10 minutes. Add hot sauce, if desired.

Enjoy.

Serves 4.

Options:
sliced mushrooms • green beans • broccoli
snow peas • sweet corn kernels

2	Tbs. vegetable oil
1	large onion, diced (about 2 cups)
1/2	medium cabbage, sliced very thin
2	stalks celery, diced
3	carrots, diced
3-4	cloves garlic, minced
1/2	red bell pepper, sliced thin
1	tsp. salt
2	pounds chicken leg quarters, rinsed
8	cups water
1/2	pound fresh greens: kale, swiss chard, spinach or collards, cut into strips
1/4	cup soy sauce
2	Tbs. fresh ginger, grated
1	tsp. sesame oil
8	oz. egg noodles
	Hot chili sauce, optional

Chicken Galangal Soup

Scott Weaner, master soup chef at White Grass for years, has shared his favorite Thai soup. You will find most of these ingredients at an Asian market. If you can't find galangal, use fresh ginger root and a dash of pepper.

4	cups coconut milk
2	stalks lemongrass, cut into 2-inch pieces and crushed
6	thin slices fresh or frozen galangal (a Southeast Asian type of ginger)
1	pound boneless, skinless chicken breast, cut into 1-inch cubes
4	Kaffir lime leaves (center vein removed)
6	small red or green chili peppers, crushed
2	Tbs. fish sauce
2	Tbs. lime juice
	Fresh cilantro for garnish

Heat coconut milk over medium heat in a soup pot until gently simmering. Add lemongrass, galangal and simmer, uncovered, 5 minutes or until fragrant.

Add chicken and bring to a boil over medium-high heat. Reduce to medium and stir. Cook for 3 to 4 minutes or until chicken is just firm.

Stir in lime leaves and chilies. Continue to cook for 2 more minutes.

Stir in fish sauce and lime juice just before serving. Garnish with chopped cilantro.

Makes 4 servings.

Grandma's Wild Mushroom Soup

Every Christmas Eve, the Gwyer family celebrates with homemade pierogies and this soup. It is a delicious tradition we look forward to all year. Instead of using dried pasta, we make tiny dough balls with leftovers from the pierogies. MBG

Chop vegetables.

Heat a stock pot over medium-high heat and add 1 Tbs. oil. Add onions and sauté 5 minutes, stirring occasionally. Add celery, carrots and garlic, cook for 3 more minutes.

Add 1 Tbs. oil and fresh mushrooms. Stir and sauté 3 to 4 minutes.

Add broth, salt and pepper.

Chop dried mushrooms into small pieces and add to pot. Reduce heat to low and simmer for about 1½ hours.

Add parsley and orzo. Simmer 10 minutes and serve.

Serves 6.

2	Tbs. olive oil
1½	cups onion, chopped
1	cup celery, chopped
1	cup carrots, chopped
2	cloves garlic, minced
8	oz. fresh button mushrooms, sliced thin
4	oz. fresh shitake or oyster mushrooms, sliced
10	cups broth (see page 33)
1	tsp. salt
¼	tsp. black pepper
1	cup dried wild mushrooms (shitake, porcini, morel, or a combination)
¼	cup fresh parsley, chopped
½	cup orzo or other very small pasta

Vegetarian Hot & Sour Soup

A cafe customer gave me this recipe on a little piece of paper. I've carried it around for years and make it every winter when I get a craving for Hot and Sour Soup. LKL

8	cups vegetable broth (see page 33)
½	cup dry wild mushroom pieces
1	cup sliced white mushrooms, shitakes or a combination
½	tsp. black pepper
1	pound firm tofu, cut into 2-inch strips
2	Tbs. cornstarch
6	green onions, diced
3	Tbs. rice vinegar
¼	cup cider vinegar
2	Tbs. sesame oil
2	eggs beaten
3	Tbs. fresh parsley, chopped
	Dash of hot sauce or cayenne powder
	Soy sauce to taste
	Extra parsley and chopped green onion

Pour the broth into a soup pot and add all mushrooms, pepper and tofu. Heat to simmering.

Remove ¼ cup of broth and dissolve cornstarch in it. Then add onion, vinegars, sesame oil and slowly add cornstarch while stirring.

Continue to cook and thicken the soup. Just before serving stir in egg, parsley, hot sauce and soy sauce to taste.

Add more hot sauce if you like it really hot. Add more vinegar if you like it really tangy.

Garnish with parsley and onion before serving.

Serves 6.

Wild Rice & Mushroom Soup

My Mom, Jeanette, gave me this recipe. I credit her with my cooking smarts. She can make any recipe taste great. LKL

In a soup pot, over medium-high heat, sauté garlic, onion, and mushrooms in butter. Cook until the onion starts to brown; this makes a flavorful broth for soup.

Add milk, cream, and chicken broth; reduce to medium low heat.

Add thyme, wild rice, chicken and sherry. Slowly simmer until soup starts to thicken. Stir often to prevent scorching.

Adjust flavor with salt and pepper. Add more broth if needed.

Enjoy on a cold day with warm bread.

Serves 4.

2	Tbs. butter
2	cloves garlic, minced
½	cup onion, chopped
8	oz. mushrooms, sliced
1	cup milk
½	cup heavy cream
1	cup chicken broth
1	tsp. thyme
2	cups cooked wild rice
2	cups cooked chopped chicken
3	Tbs. sherry
	Salt and pepper

Chicken, Rice, & Broccoli Soup

4	chicken leg quarters
1	tsp. salt
4	quarts water
1½	cups onion, chopped
2	cloves garlic, minced
1	cup uncooked Basmati rice
1	(10 oz.) pkg. frozen chopped broccoli or 2 cups fresh florets
2–4	cups milk
1	tsp. thyme
½	tsp. salt
¼	tsp. black pepper

Cook chicken in salted water in a large soup pot about 20 minutes. Remove from water to cool and save broth in another container. When cooled, remove skin and pick meat from the bone and cut into bite-sized pieces. Set chicken aside.

Reheat the soup pot. Add ¼ cup stock and sauté onion, garlic, and rice together until onion is tender. Then add 3 cups of chicken broth and continue cooking, covered, until rice is steamed, about 15 minutes.

After rice is cooked add broccoli, milk, thyme, salt and pepper.

Continue to cook until broccoli is tender. Add chopped chicken and more broth or milk to desired consistency.

Serves 4 to 6.

Option: ½ cup cooked wild rice adds more texture and color to this soup if you have it.

Butternut, Fennel & Leek Purée

This is a velvety, smooth soup that serves as an excellent starter to a meal. It's an awesome recipe from my favorite brother, David. MBG

Peel squash, remove seeds and dice into 1-inch pieces. Take care when cutting; winter squash are very dense.

Cut base off fennel and remove stalks. Cut bulb into quarters.

Trim off roots of leeks, leaving about 1 inch of white and remove dark green leaves. Leave tender white and pale green parts. Cut leeks into 1-inch slices and soak in a bowl of water. Rinse well to remove all sand and dirt. Remove from water.

In a soup pot, heat oil and butter and sauté vegetables for 15 minutes, stirring occasionally. Add salt, pepper and broth. Simmer for 30 minutes. Cool slightly and purée in a blender or food processor.

Serves 4 to 6.

1	large butternut squash
1	bulb fennel
1	bunch leeks
2	Tbs. olive oil
2	Tbs. butter
½	tsp. salt
½	tsp. black pepper
6	cups vegetarian broth

Roasted Yellow Pepper Soup with Shrimp

This is a combination of two soups from two of my favorite cooks, Laurie and my brother, David. I think you will really like this one. MBG

6	yellow bell peppers
1	Tbs. olive oil
1	Tbs. butter
2	cloves garlic, chopped
2	cups onion, chopped
1	medium potato, peeled and diced
½	tsp. salt
½	tsp. black pepper
6	cups broth
1	pound, peeled, deveined, raw medium shrimp (save shells for broth)
½	cup green bell pepper, chopped
1	cup fresh tomatoes, cut in chunks
¼	cup fresh cilantro, chopped for garnish

Roast peppers by placing on a grill, or under an oven broiler and cook until black and blistered. Cool and peel away charred skin under running water. Remove seeds and stems. Set aside.

Prepare broth, see page 33. Include shrimp shells for extra flavor.

In a soup pot, sauté onion, garlic, and potato over medium heat for about 10 to 15 minutes. Add seasonings.

Chop roasted peppers and add to pot, along with broth. Simmer 30 minutes.

Purée in a blender or food processor until smooth.

Return to pot and add shrimp, green pepper and tomatoes. Simmer about 10 minutes, or until shrimp is pink.

Serve with cilantro sprinkled on top.

Serves 4 generously or 6 as an appetizer.

Southwestern Chowder

This chowder is a White Grass favorite that is very warming and satisfying to the taste buds. It's not spicy, but you can add hot sauce if you prefer.

Sauté onion in oil in a 4 quart soup pot. Add cumin, coriander, and oregano and sauté until onion is translucent. Add carrots, potatoes, and stock; simmer for 20 minutes.

In a medium skillet, sauté pepper and zucchini in oil until soft. Remove from heat.

When potatoes are cooked, remove pot from heat, retaining all the liquid for broth. Scoop out vegetables to a food processor and purée adding a little broth if necessary to blend.

Return puréed potato and carrot mixture back to broth in pot and add zucchini, pepper, corn, salsa, cream cheese, cheddar cheese, and salt and pepper. Stir well to blend cheeses and vegetables.

Continue to heat on low to prevent scorching until all the cheese is melted.

Garnish with cilantro and enjoy.

Serves 6.

2	Tbs. oil
3	cups onion, chopped
1	tsp. cumin
1	tsp. coriander
1	tsp. oregano
1/2	cup carrots, diced
1	pound sweet potatoes, peeled and cubed
1	pound white potatoes, cubed
4	cups water or stock
1	(10 oz.) package frozen corn
1	Tbs. oil
1	small jalapeno pepper, seeded and minced
1/2	cup zucchini, diced
1	cup salsa, fresh or commercially prepared
4	oz. cream cheese
3/4	cups cheddar cheese, grated
	Salt and pepper to taste
3	Tbs. fresh cilantro

Morgan's Turkey Noodle Soup

Another great use of leftovers. Morgan Chase made this for us.

1 turkey breast, cooked or 3 lbs. turkey parts, raw

1 Tbs. olive oil or 1 Tbs. butter

2 cups onion, chopped

1 cup celery, chopped

1 cup carrots

1 Tbs. butter or oil

1 tsp. herbes de provence*

½ pound dry egg noodles

Salt and pepper to taste

In an 8-quart soup pot, boil turkey carcass, or raw parts in 6 quarts of salted water to make broth, for about 20 minutes. Remove and cool. Separate meat from bones and set aside.

If already using cooked meat, chop 3 cups and set aside.

Sauté onion, celery, and carrots in a smaller pan in butter or oil.

While this cooks, heat broth to boiling in soup pot.

Add the vegetable mixture to the broth along with the herbes de provence.

Once the broth is boiling, add the dry noodles. Adjust seasonings and cook for 10 to 15 minutes, depending on their size; larger noodles take longer to cook.

Add reserved meat to the soup and more water if necessary. Adjust seasonings and serve.

Serves 4 to 6.

*Herbes de Provence is a delicate French blend of thyme, rosemary, savory, tarragon and basil.

Potato & Leek Soup

This is smooth and rich, perfect for a start to dinner. A nice addition is to add flaked smoked fish before serving.

Slice root end off leek. Peel away dark green layers. Slice leek lengthwise and fan layers out under running water to remove all sand and dirt. Keep tender white and pale green parts, chop.

Heat a large soup pot over medium-high heat. Add oil and butter then onion and garlic, cook 2 minutes.

Add leeks and sauté 3 more minutes, or until veggies just begin to brown.

Add potatoes and toss with flour and salt. Pour in water and simmer over medium-low heat for 20 minutes, stirring occasionally until potatoes are tender.

Briefly purée or pulse in a food processor. Return to pot and stir in milk and cream, simmer another 10 minutes.

Serves 6.

1	large bunch leeks
1	Tbs. olive oil
1	Tbs. butter
1	large onion, chopped (2 cups)
2	cloves garlic, minced
2½	pounds red potatoes, peeled and cubed
¼	cup flour
3½	cups water
½	tsp. salt
3	cups milk
1	cup heavy cream

Salads

Antipasto Salad

Laurie's Tofu Salad

Green Bean Insalata

Broccoli Salad

Edamame Salad

Southwest Bean Salad

Pily's Black Bean and Rice Salad

Rice Salad with French Vinaigrette

Benny's Rabbit Slaw

Deb's Summer Salad

M.B.'s Painted Salad

Flank Steak Salad

Calamari Salad

Bruce's Spinach and Pear Salad

Cranberry Vinaigrette

Mountain Maple Vinaigrette

Singapore Splash Dressing

Antipasto Salad

Panini Queen Mike Stinson makes one mean antipasto salad. This is a quick recipe because there is very little chopping involved.

Toss vegetables and cheese in a large bowl.

Add marinade. Stir well to combine flavors.

Let set for one hour before serving.

Serves 8.

Options: sliced green pepper • yellow pepper cucumber chunks • canned baby corn

2	(16 oz.) cans artichoke hearts, drained and quartered
1	(6 oz.) can black olives, drained
1	small jar green olives, drained
1	pint cherry tomatoes
1	cup green beans (blanched or canned)
4	oz. crumbled feta cheese
2	(16 oz.) jars marinated mushrooms (save the marinade)
1	(16 oz.) can of kidney beans, drained
1	cup carrot sticks

Marinade:

1/4	cup olive oil
2	Tbs. balsamic vinegar
2	Tbs. garlic, minced
	Dash of Worcestershire sauce
	Dash of soy sauce
	Black pepper to taste
1/4	cup mushroom marinade (reserved)

49

Laurie's Tofu Salad

Here is a quick and easy vegetarian sandwich or spread.

1	pound firm tofu
4	green onions, chopped
2	Tbs. pickle relish
1	rib of celery chopped
2	Tbs. sweet red pepper, chopped
2	tsp. Dijon mustard
1/3	cup mayonnaise
1/4	tsp. dill weed
2	Tbs. fresh parsley, chopped
	Dash of salt and pepper

Remove tofu from package. Place on a dinner plate. Add another plate on top. Set a heavy object on that plate (5# bag of sugar or a gallon of milk). Let set about 20 minutes; water will drain from tofu.

Crumble the tofu.

Combine all ingredients and serve on sandwiches, pita or crackers.

A great vegetarian alternative to egg salad.

Tofu is a soy product, very high in protein, that was developed in China over 1,000 years ago. It is made from soy milk that is curdled and pressed. You will usually find two types—firm or silken, both sold refrigerated near the produce section of most groceries.

Firm tofu can be sliced or diced and used in soups, salads, stews and stir fry. It can be grilled or baked. On it's own, it has little flavor but it easily takes on the taste of whatever it is prepared with.

Silken tofu is more delicate. It can be puréed to a yogurt-like consistency to use in creamy soups, sauces, dressings, dips and puddings.

Try tofu as a healthy alternative to meat—or combine it with meat to add nutritional value to your meals.

Green Bean Insalata

If you have a plethora of green beans, this is a covered dish delight.

Steam or blanch beans to desired tenderness, then cool in cold water. Drain well.

Combine oil, juice and pepper. Add beans, toss to coat with oil mixture. Sprinkle on dill and onion and toss again.

Allow beans to marinate for 30 minutes or cover and chill for up to 4 hours.

Serve at room temperature. Just before serving, sprinkle on the cheese and tomatoes; toss again.

Makes 6 servings.

We absolutely love buying produce from our local growers. There is no better way to get fresher, cleaner, tastier ingredients. Better ingredients always make a better dish. Find the location and hours of a farmer's market near you. Support them (especially organic growers) so they can continue to provide superior products and make a living for themselves.

1   pound fresh green beans, stems and strings removed

3   Tbs. olive oil

2   Tbs. fresh lemon juice
    Fresh ground black pepper to taste

2   Tbs. minced fresh dill

3   Tbs. red onion, sliced very thin

1/3   cup crumbled feta cheese

1   pint cherry or grape tomatoes

Broccoli Salad

Bacon can be left out to make this a tasty vegetarian salad.

2 bunches of broccoli, cut into bite sized pieces

1/4 cup red onion, cut in 1-inch thin slices

1/2 cup cashews

1/2 cup raisins

1/2 pound bacon, cooked until crisp and crumbled

Place broccoli and onion in a bowl. Prepare dressing and toss. Then add cashews, raisins, and bacon. Stir again. Serve the same day.

Serves 4 to 6.

Dressing:

4 Tbs. cider vinegar

1/2 cup sugar

Pinch of salt

1/2 tsp. dry mustard

1/2 cup vegetable oil

Pour first four ingredients into food processor or blender. Slowly add oil to emulsify dressing while machine is running.

Edamame Salad

This is an attempt to recreate an amazing salad I had in Peru. I asked for the ingredients, but since I speak Spanish like Tarzan, this is an instinctual guess.
It tastes pretty good anyway. MB

Cook edamame in 2 cups boiling water with salt for about 8 minutes, drain and cool.

Mix in a bowl with peppers, onion, cilantro, garlic and cucumber.

In a small separate bowl, whisk together oil, vinegar, lime juice and spices. Pour over salad, chill at least half an hour and serve.

Serves 4.

Edamame are immature soybeans that are picked green and served fresh, steamed in the pods or shelled. They look like lima beans but have more protein and a firmer texture. Buy them, usually frozen, at Asian or International markets.

1	pound shelled frozen edamame beans
1/2	tsp. salt
1	medium red bell pepper, diced
1/2	cup red or sweet onion, diced
1/3	cup fresh cilantro, chopped
1	small cucumber, peeled and diced
2	cloves garlic, minced
1	jalapeno, seeded and minced
3	Tbs. canola oil
2	Tbs. cider vinegar
1/4	cup fresh lime juice
1/2	tsp. salt
1/2	tsp. black pepper
1/2	tsp. ground cumin
1/2	tsp. chili powder

Southwest Bean Salad

Former Canaan Valley resident Jan Corrin shared this recipe with us and it is very popular during the summer catering season.

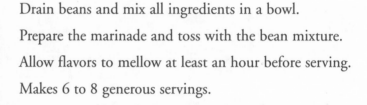

1	(15 oz.) can white beans such as navy or cannelloni
1	(15 oz.) can black beans
1	(15 oz.) can pinto beans
1	(4 oz.) can green chiles
1	cup celery, chopped
1	cup green onion, chopped
1/2	cup green bell pepper, chopped
1/2	cup sweet red bell pepper, chopped

Marinade:

2	Tbs. lime juice
1/3	cup olive oil
1/4	cup cider vinegar
2	cloves garlic, minced
2	Tbs. cilantro, chopped
1 1/2	tsp. chili powder
1 1/2	tsp. cumin
	Dash of cayenne

Drain beans and mix all ingredients in a bowl.

Prepare the marinade and toss with the bean mixture.

Allow flavors to mellow at least an hour before serving.

Makes 6 to 8 generous servings.

Pily's Black Bean & Rice Salad

Pily Henderson has provided us with some wonderful Mexican recipes from her home country. This is a new cafe favorite.

Place the first 7 ingredients in a bowl, reserving the avocados until later.

Mix dressing by whisking all ingredients in a small bowl and pour over salad.

Then gently stir in the avocados and serve with tortilla chips or pita bread.

Plentifully serves 6 to 8.

2   (15 oz.) cans black beans, drained and rinsed

2   cups cooked white rice (Basmati is best)

1   cup shredded mozzarella cheese

1   cup red onion, sliced into thin 1-inch pieces

3   Roma tomatoes, diced

1   cup cilantro, chopped

1   jalapeño, seeded and minced

2   small avocados, cubed

Dressing:

¼   cup olive oil

¼   cup red wine vinegar

1   tsp. oregano

2   cloves garlic, minced

1   Tbs. sugar

    Juice of one lemon

Rice Salad with French Vinaigrette

For a simple salad, this is exceptionally good and a great party dish.

2   cups white rice*

¼   cup chopped green pepper

¼   cup chopped celery

10   halved black olives

Optional: ¼ tsp dried or 1 Tbs. fresh basil or fresh parsley chopped,

¼   cup of the following vinaigrette recipe:

French Vinaigrette

¼   tsp. salt

¼   tsp. pepper

½   cup olive oil

2   Tbs. fresh lemon juice

¼   tsp. dry mustard

1   clove garlic crushed

Cook rice, according to package directions. While rice is warm, mix in peppers, celery, olives and herbs.

To make vinaigrette, blend all ingredients in a jar and store in refrigerator until ready for use. Shake well before tossing with salad.

Garnish salad with halved cherry tomatoes.

Served best at room temperature.

Serves 4 to 6.

*For a different twist, add ½ cup cooked wild rice.

Benny's Rabbit Slaw

Our favorite cooks usually have several specialities. This is definitely one of Ben McKean's. He created it especially for his fresh garden vegetables. You'll love it.

Slice and grate vegetables. Toss in a large bowl.

For dressing, whisk mayo, miso, vinegar, soy sauce, and tahini. Stir in spices. Toss with vegetables.

Serves 4 to 6 healthy hungry eaters.

1	small or $\frac{1}{2}$ medium cabbage, sliced very thin
2	carrots, grated
1	medium raw beet, peeled and grated
$\frac{1}{2}$	medium onion, sliced very thin
$\frac{1}{4}$	cup fresh parsley, chopped
$\frac{1}{2}$	cup mayonnaise (or mayo substitute)
1	Tbs. sweet white miso (or $\frac{1}{2}$ Tbs. brown miso)
2	Tbs. cider vinegar
1	Tbs. soy sauce or Bragg Liquid Aminos
1	Tbs. tahini
$\frac{1}{2}$	tsp. salt
$\frac{1}{2}$	tsp. fresh ground black pepper
$\frac{1}{4}$	tsp. celery seed
	Dash of ground cumin

Deb's Summer Salad

Our longtime friend and White Grasser, Deb Klein, is an amazing salad maker. She always combines flavors and textures to produce unforgettable meals. This is a chance to embrace your creativity and make the most of the fresh ingredients you have on hand. Use whatever sounds or looks good to you and it will be unforgettable.

½ **pound mixed salad greens**

½ **cup toasted nuts (walnuts, pecans, or pumpkin seeds)**

½ **cup of at least two kinds of fruit (blueberries, diced apples or pears, dried cranberries, diced melons, pomegranate seeds, strawberries, oranges or grapes)**

½ **cup cheese (feta, blue, smoked gouda, or goat)**

2 **carrots, grated**

⅓ **cup sweet onions, diced**

⅓ **cup red or yellow bell pepper, diced**

1 **cup grape tomatoes**

Balsamic Dijon Vinaigrette

1 **cup balsamic vinegar**

1 **tsp. sugar**

2 **Tbs. Dijon mustard**

1 **clove garlic, finely minced**

¾ **cup olive oil**

"Beef up" this salad to make it a meal on its own by adding grilled salmon, chicken, beef or tofu.

In a large bowl toss salad ingredients.

Prepare vinaigrette.

Toss to coat.

Serves 2 as a meal or 4 as a side dish.

Balsamic Dijon Vinaigrette

Combine first four ingredients in a bowl. Drizzle in olive oil while whisking to blend. Store in a jar for up to two weeks in the fridge.

MB's Painted Salad

This is a most beautiful salad — but not too beautiful to eat. The colors look like a painter's palate and the beet dressing is really eye catching. The tangy taste of the feta really compliments the dressing.

Assembly of this salad is pretty simple, just combine all ingredients in a large bowl, toss gently and top with dressing.

Serves 2 to 4.

4	oz. organic salad greens
1	cup grated carrots
1	cup grape tomatoes
1/2	yellow bell pepper, sliced
1/2	cup feta cheese, crumbled
3	oz. smoked turkey, sliced in strips

Dressing:

Cook beets by boiling or steaming until knife tender. Or roast in an oven, wrapped in foil at 350°F for 50 minutes. Cool and peel skin off beets.

Combine all ingredients in a food processor and blend until smooth. Store in refrigerator in glass jar. It will keep for two weeks.

If necessary, you can use canned beets, although the flavor and color won't be quite the same.

Beet Dressing

1	large bunch of beets (one pound)
2	cloves garlic
1	Tbs. onion, chopped
1/4	tsp. salt
1/2	cup cider vinegar
1/2	cup mayonnaise

Flank Steak Salad

Prepare this for a quick summer dinner. The addition of meat makes this salad a full meal. You'll be very satisfied.

1	(2 pound) flank steak
	Bottled Italian dressing
10	oz. of mixed salad greens
1	medium red onion, sliced very thin
1/2	pound steamed green beans
1	(15 oz.) can garbanzo beans, rinsed
1	(15 oz.) jar pickled beets, sliced
1	pint cherry or grape tomatoes
1	cup blue cheese
	Mountain Maple Vinaigrette (see page 64)

Marinate steak in ½ cup Italian dressing while preparing grill.

Cook over medium-high heat quickly, only 4 to 6 minutes on each side depending on the thickness of the steak. Meat should be pink in the center. Remove from grill and let steak set for about 5 minutes.

Slice, across the grain at a diagonal into thin strips.

Make salad by combining greens and vegetables, toss. Plate up salad, and place sliced steak on top. Finish with crumbled blue cheese.

Make large salad servings and this will be a meal for four.

Calamari Salad

We sauté calamari in a smooth wine sauce and present it over a bed of romaine on a large platter when entertaining. It could be a meal when served with some heavy hors d'oeuvres.

Rinse squid and cut into pieces. Use body and tentacles. Discard any hard or cartilage pieces.

In a large skillet, heat olive oil over medium-high heat. Add onion and garlic and sauté until lightly browned, about 4 minutes.

Add wine and sundried tomato bits. Add calamari. Cook 2 to 3 minutes, remove from heat.

Add salt, pepper and oregano, stir.

Arrange chopped romaine on a platter or individual plates. Pour calamari and sauce over lettuce. Scatter salads with olives and tomatoes. Serve immediately.

Serves 4.

Buy calamari (squid) frozen, at an Asian or large grocery. Do not thaw until the day you cook it. Cook at high heat quickly—only 2 to 3 minutes to keep it tender.

1	pound calamari (squid), cleaned and diced
1	Tbs. olive oil
1/4	cup onion, minced
2	cloves garlic, minced
1/2	cup dry white wine
1	Tbs. sundried tomatoes, finely chopped
1/4	tsp. salt
1/4	tsp. fresh ground black pepper
1/8	tsp. oregano
1	head romaine lettuce, chopped
1/4	cup Calamata olives, minced
1/2	pint grape tomatoes, halved

Bruce's Spinach & Pear Salad

This recipe is from Chip's brother-in-law, from Bennington, VT, who is an excellent cook.

½	(10 oz.) bag baby spinach
½	(10 oz.) bag spring mix
¼	red onion cut in 1 inch pieces
1	red pear, sliced
¼	cup walnuts or pine nuts, toasted*
¼	cup blue cheese, crumbled
3	Tbs. Balsamic vinegar
3	Tbs. olive oil
	Salt and pepper to taste

Toss greens, onion, pear, nuts and cheese in a salad bowl.

Combine vinegar, oil, and salt and pepper in a jar and shake.

Toss dressing into salad just before serving.

Serves 4.

*To toast nuts: Place nuts in a dry sauté pan on medium high heat.

Stir constantly until they begin to brown and give off their aroma.

Remove from pan to prevent burning.

Cranberry Vinaigrette

Only true friends share the location of their berry picking spots with you, but our friend, Mary Anders did share this recipe with us.

Purée cranberries in a food processor or blender.

Add the vinegar and dry ingredients.

Slowly add the oil until well blended. Serve on tossed salad.

¼ cup fresh cranberries
½ cup sugar
½ tsp. dry mustard
1 tsp. salt
⅓ cup apple cider vinegar
1 small clove of garlic, chopped
1 cup salad oil

We love **cranberries.** They grow wild here in high elevation bogs. A quintessential autumn Canaan Valley outing is leaf peeping, picnicking and cranberry picking.

Mountain Maple Vinaigrette

Erin and Pete Cozzi served this at their wedding in Vermont. It's been the house favorite at the cafe ever since.

$1/2$	cup maple syrup
$1/4$	cup red wine vinegar
$1/4$	cup balsamic vinegar
$1/4$	cup soy sauce
1	Tbs. minced onion
2	tsp. minced garlic
1	Tbs. Dijon mustard
1	cup extra virgin olive oil
1	cup vegetable oil
	Salt and pepper to taste

Process syrup, vinegars, & soy sauce in food processor until combined. Add onion, garlic, mustard. With machine running, slowly add oil. Process until emulsified (does not separate). Stir in salt and pepper.

This recipe can be served on your favorite salad greens and will quickly become a necessity of life.

As someone who has actually made maple syrup,
I respect the time and hard work that goes into every drop. It takes 40 gallons of sap and at least 24 hours of labor to make a gallon of that golden sweet tree nectar.
It's worth $100 a gallon to me. MBG

Singapore Splash Dressing

Cooking for others can be interesting because of those you meet along the way. This recipe is from Lorelei Verlee from Kokomo, Indiana. I met her at a catering in Canaan Valley and she shared this salad dressing with us. LKL

Mix all together for a refreshing new salad dressing.

Lorelei recommended this dressing on a salad of mesclun mix, dried cherries, toasted walnuts, and dry sautéed pears.

$1/2$	cup olive oil
1	cup balsamic vinegar
$1/4$	orange juice
2	tsp. fresh ground ginger
2	tsp. lemon zest
2	Tbs. sugar

Side Dishes

Asian Greens

Annie's Burnt Greens

Greens with Currants and Pine Nuts

Roman Style Greens

Creamed Spinach

Sauté of Zucchini, Squash and Carrots

Maize de Mejico

Marinated Green Beans

Ginger Broccoli

Roasted Asparagus

Asparagus and Mushroom Grits

Yellow Rice

Cilantro Rice

Potato Latkes

Garlic Mashed Potatoes

Quinoa with Shitake Pate

Mojito Squash

Asian Greens

At the cafe, cooked greens are one of our favorite side dishes.

Using a wok, sauté garlic in oil for about one minute.

Add greens and stir-fry about one minute.

Add remaining ingredients except for soy sauce. Stir-fry until greens are tender.

Toss with soy sauce just before serving.

Makes 4 servings.

2	Tbs. vegetable oil
2	cloves garlic, minced
1	pound fresh kale, collards, or bok choy, fresh, chopped
1/4	cup Chinese rice wine or sherry
1	tsp. ginger root, fresh grated
1	Tbs. lemon juice
1	tsp. sugar
2	Tbs. water
2	Tbs. soy sauce

Annie's Burnt Greens

This recipe comes from my sister, Anne Hart, who has great taste and always has a few new, exciting recipes up her sleeve. LKL

1   bunch of kale or collard greens
¼   cup white wine
¼   cup water
1   Tbs. lemon juice
    Salt and pepper to taste
3   Tbs. olive oil
1-2 cloves minced garlic

Pick through greens and pull off stems. Tear into pieces.

In a large pot, add wine, water and lemon. Heat until almost boiling and add greens, simmer about 10 minutes, stirring occasionally.

Drain liquid from pan and season greens with salt and pepper.

Spread into a shallow lightly oiled baking dish and drizzle with oil and garlic.

Bake at 350°F until the top and edges become crispy; about 15 to 20 minutes.

Serve as a bed for rice and Teriyaki Fish, page 159.

Serves 4.

Greens with Currants & Pine Nuts

Yet another great greens recipe.

Cover currants in hot water to plump them.

Tear kale and chard leaves away from stems. Discard stems and cut leaves into 2 to 3 inch ribbons. Wash greens and dry them in a salad spinner.

Heat oil in a large sauté pan. Add kale, garlic, water and a pinch of salt and pepper.

Sauté for one minute. Add chard and cook 5 minutes, until the greens are just tender. Lower heat, add butter, currants and pine nuts. Cook 2 to 3 minutes.

Season with salt and pepper.

Serves up to 6.

1	Tbs. diced currants
1/4	cup hot water
6	cups fresh kale
6	cups red or green Swiss chard
1	Tbs. light olive oil
1	garlic clove, finely chopped
1/4	cup water
	Salt and pepper to taste
2	Tbs. butter
1	Tbs. pine nuts, toasted

Roman Style Greens

Chris Leon Pellicoro gave us her father-in-law's great greens recipe.

2 Tbs. olive oil

1 medium onion, chopped

4 cloves garlic, minced

1 (28 oz.) can diced tomatoes with juice

2 pounds fresh greens cleaned (kale, swiss chard, beet, collards, mustard–your preference)

1 tsp. dried oregano

1 tsp. dried basil

1 tsp. salt

½ tsp. black pepper

Heat a large pot over medium heat, add oil. Then add onions and garlic. Sauté until lightly browned, about 5 minutes.

Add tomatoes, cook 8 to 10 minutes.

Add greens and cover with a lid. Simmer on low for 15 minutes then add spices.

Serve with cooked pasta, mashed potatoes or rice.

Serves 6 to 8.

Creamed Spinach

This is an easy and colorful side dish that goes well with fish and meat.

Cook spinach in one inch of boiling, salted water in a large pot, covered. Stir once or twice until wilted, 1 to 2 minutes.

Drain in a colander; cool slightly and squeeze out the rest of the water. Chop spinach coarsely.

Cook onion in butter in a small heavy bottomed saucepan over low heat; about 4 minutes. Whisk in flour and stir constantly about 2 minutes. Add warm milk and continue to stir. Simmer sauce about 4 minutes, stirring to prevent scorching.

Add Parmesan, salt and pepper to taste. Add spinach and stir in until just heated.

Serves 4.

Note: One 10-ounce package of thawed and squeezed frozen chopped spinach can be used if fresh spinach is unavailable.

1 ½ **pounds baby spinach**

½ **small onion, chopped finely**

2 **Tbs. butter**

2 **Tbs. all-purpose flour**

1 **cup plus 2 Tbs. milk, warmed**

2 **Tbs. freshly grated Parmesan cheese (optional)**

Salt and pepper to taste

73

Sauté of Zucchini, Squash & Carrots

A very beautiful mélange of vegetables, this is an excellent summer side dish.

1   medium zucchini
2   carrots
1   medium yellow squash
½   medium onion, chopped
2-3 cloves garlic, minced
2   Tbs. olive oil
½   tsp. salt
¼   tsp. black pepper

Wash and grate zucchini, carrots and squash.

Heat a heavy large skillet over medium heat for one minute, add oil, wait another minute. Sauté onions for 3 minutes. Add remaining veggies and garlic.

Cook until desired doneness, stirring occasionally, for 5 to 7 minutes. Season.

Serves 4 to 6.

Another attractive presentation is to slice veggies into wide ribbons using a vegetable peeler.

Maize de Mejico

Dear friend and former White Grass kitchen chick, Deborah Klein got this recipe from her amigo. The sauce for this recipe is incredible. Don't limit yourself to using it just on corn. It is an excellent topping for grilled fish, shrimp, chicken, veggie burgers, mushrooms, quesadillas....

Remove silk from each ear of corn, leaving husk. Soak in cold water for 30 minutes.

Meanwhile, blend mayo, zest, chili powder, pepper and cilantro and mix well.

Place corn on a hot grill and roast for about 20 minutes, turning occasionally. Peel off husks and brush with mayo topping. Cut lime into quarters and offer a wedge for squeezing over corn.

Serves 4.

Tip–If grilling is out of the question, steam shucked corn about 5 minutes, then serve with sauce and lime.

*For information about zest, see page 99.

4	ears fresh corn
½	cup mayonnaise
	Zest* of one large lime
½	tsp. chili powder
½	tsp. black pepper
3	tsp. cilantro, minced

Marinated Green Beans

Perfect as a cool summer side dish or an elegant hors d'oeuvre.

2	pounds fresh green beans
I	medium onion, sliced very thin
I	lemon, sliced very thin
I	clove garlic, finely minced
1/2	tsp. black pepper
I	tsp. salt
I	tsp. sugar
3/4	cup vegetable oil
3/4	cup white vinegar
1/2	tsp. red pepper flakes (optional)

Trim, rinse and steam green beans to desired doneness. Cool.

In a large shallow bowl, mix remaining ingredients. Add green beans and toss.

Chill at least one hour and up to one and a half days.

Serve chilled or at room temperature.

Serves 8 to 10.

We rave about our pot luck dinners. They're always a surprise; you never know what you're going to get. Once, at Ruthie's baby shower, everyone brought green bean dishes. Luckily, they were all different recipes. Sometimes it's good to tell people what to bring.

Ginger Broccoli

Candied ginger gives a touch of sweetness to this recipe. It's a nice balance for the soy sauce.

Cut broccoli into bite sized pieces.

Slice ginger into skinny strips then in half.

Heat skillet or wok over medium-high heat. Add oil, wait one minute. Add broccoli and stir fry about 2 minutes. Add ginger and soy sauce. Cook another 2 minutes.

Plate up immediately.

Serves 6.

*If candied ginger is not available, use fresh, peeled, sliced ginger.

1	bunch broccoli
1	Tbs. vegetable oil
2	pieces (2 Tbs.) crystallized or candied ginger*
1	Tbs. soy sauce

Roasted Asparagus

Roasting vegetables is an excellent way to enhance flavor while preserving nutrients. Try this method for cooking carrots, brussel sprouts, fennel, onions, parsnips, rutabagas and turnips. Roasting time will be longer for dense vegetables.

2   pounds asparagus
2   Tbs. extra virgin olive oil
1   Tbs. balsamic vinegar
    Salt and pepper

Preheat oven to 450°F.

Snap off bottom ends of asparagus. Rinse.

Toss with oil and vinegar on a baking sheet. Sprinkle with salt and pepper.

Bake about 10 minutes.

Serves 6 to 8.

Asparagus and Mushroom Grits

Grits have certainly come a long way from plain old breakfast food. These will "class up" any meat or fish dish – and can stand on their own as a veggie dinner.

Slowly stir grits and salt into boiling water. Reduce heat to medium-low and cover. Cook 5 to 7 minutes or until thickened, stirring occasionally. Remove pan from heat and keep warm until vegetables are ready.

Trim asparagus and cut into 1-inch pieces.

Cook the onion in olive oil in a skillet over medium heat for 1 minute, stirring constantly. Add the asparagus, mushrooms, thyme, salt and pepper. Cook for 3 minutes, stirring constantly.

Stir in wine and cook, covered, for 2 minutes.

Place grits into a shallow serving bowl and stir in ¼ cup of Parmesan cheese.

Spoon vegetables and wine over grits and garnish with more Parmesan and lemon zest. Enjoy hot.

Serves 6 as a side dish or 4 as a main course.

1	cup quick grits
4	cups water
½	tsp. salt
1	pound fresh asparagus
½	sweet onion, thin sliced in 2 inch strips
3	Tbs. olive oil
1	pound mushrooms, cut in half
2	tsp. dried thyme or 2 Tbs. fresh thyme
½	tsp. salt
⅓	tsp. fresh ground pepper
½	cup dry white wine
	Parmesan cheese
1	tsp. grated lemon zest

Yellow Rice

With an Asian flair, this is a great side dish for many of the fish or chicken recipes in this book.

4½ cups water

1 cup sweetened flaked coconut

2½ tsp. ground turmeric

Peel from one lemon (yellow part only)*

1 thin slice of fresh ginger

1 bay leaf

2 tsp. salt

2½ cups white or basmati rice

Bring water to boil with all ingredients, except rice, in a 4-quart saucepan.

Stir in rice and reduce to low heat and cook covered for 20 to 25 minutes.

Remove lemon peel, ginger, and bay leaf. Fluff rice with a fork before serving.

Serves 8.

*Use a vegetable peeler and remove skin from lemon in big wide strips. Avoid using the bitter white pith.

To have fresh **ginger** on hand at all times, keep it in a sealed bag in the freezer for months. Take out as much as you need, peel and grate it into your favorite dishes.

Cilantro Rice

Another Mexican specialty from Pily Henderson.

Sauté garlic, onion and rice in oil. When onions are tender, add tomatoes. Sauté for 2 minutes more.

Add broth, carrots, peas, salt and the cilantro.

Mix well, cover the pot and cook on medium heat. Don't stir any more; just let the rice steam. When all the liquid is evaporated, the rice is done (about 20 minutes).

Serves 6.

1	Tbs. olive oil
2	cloves garlic, minced
1	large onion, minced
2	cups white rice, uncooked
1	can chopped tomatoes or 1 cup fresh chopped tomato
4	cups chicken broth or vegetable broth
2	carrots, chopped in small cubes
1	cup frozen peas
1/2	tsp. salt
1 1/2	cups fresh cilantro, chopped

Potato Latkes

This traditional Jewish side dish can be made ahead and kept warm in the oven until serving. Check out the sweet potato option below.

2 **pounds red potatoes (about 10 small potatoes)**

½ **tsp. salt**

½ **medium onion, grated**

¼ **cup flour**

1 **tsp. baking powder**

1 **tsp. salt**

 Fresh ground black pepper

2 **eggs**

¼ **cup fresh chopped parsley**

 Vegetable oil for frying

Grate potatoes in a large bowl, fill with cold water and ½ tsp. salt.

In a separate bowl, grate onion and mix with flour, baking powder, salt, pepper and eggs. Drain potatoes and add onion mixture. Mix well and add parsley.

Heat a large skillet over medium heat, add 1 Tbs. of oil. Form patties by placing several spoonfuls of potato into skillet and cook until golden brown on both sides (about 4 minutes on each side).

Continue to add a little oil as needed until all cakes are cooked. Keep warm in a low temperature oven until serving. Sour cream and applesauce are traditional accompaniments.

Makes enough for 6 to 8 people.

Variation—Try this recipe with sweet potatoes instead of red potatoes. Add a little garlic and 1 tsp. curry powder to jazz them up.

Garlic Mashed Potatoes

Some meals must be served with mashed potatoes. These are not your average potatoes — they're fancied up a bit for more flavor.

Boil potatoes in salted water in a large covered pot, about 30 minutes.

While potatoes are cooking, sauté garlic in another pan in 1 tablespoon of butter for about 1 minute. Remove from heat.

Drain liquid when ready to mash potatoes, saving liquid for soup broth if needed for your next meal.

In the pot with the potatoes, place garlic, butter, sour cream and cream cheese. Use mixer or hand masher to mash with milk to achieve consistency you like. Salt and pepper to taste.

Serves 4 to 6.

*Another option is to add sautéed onions and shredded cheddar or smoked gouda cheese instead of cream cheese

8	medium sized red potatoes, peeled and cut into chunks
2	cloves garlic, peeled and minced
4	Tbs. butter
½	cup sour cream
4	oz. cream cheese
½	cup milk
	Salt and pepper to taste

We like using red potatoes for nearly any purpose. They are creamy and lower in starch so they hold up well in soups, salads and of course are excellent mashed. And you can leave the skins on if you prefer.

Quinoa with Shitake Pate

Laurie and I made this one rainy day while looking for something to do with fresh shitakes. The mushroom spread is also a great topping for bread, pizza or pasta. MBG

1   cup quinoa*
¼ tsp. salt

Shitake Pate

2	Tbs. olive oil
2	Tbs. butter
3	Tbs. onion, chopped
3	cloves garlic
1	(8 oz.) pkg. button mushrooms, sliced
¼	pound fresh shitake mushrooms, sliced
2	Tbs. white wine
1	tsp. soy sauce
¼	tsp. black pepper

Rinse quinoa well and cook, covered in a saucepan with 2 cups water and salt for 15 to 20 minutes, until all liquid is absorbed. Remove from heat and make pate.

In a skillet over medium-high heat, sauté onion in 1 Tbs. olive oil about 5 minutes. Then add garlic and cook another minute. Remove from skillet.

Add 1 Tbs. olive oil and 2 Tbs. butter to skillet and cook mushrooms over medium-high heat until browned, about 8 to 10 minutes. Remove from skillet and add wine to deglaze pan. Swish it around to get all browned bits off the pan.

Place onions, mushrooms and wine in a food processor. Add soy sauce and pepper. Blend until smooth. This can be made ahead and refrigerated or frozen.

Mix ½ cup or more of pate into the quinoa. Serve hot.

Makes enough for 4 to 6.

*Quinoa (pronounced keen-wa) is an ancient food from the Andes mountains. Considered to be a grain, it is really a seed from a spinach-like plant. It is very nutritious and high in protein. It has a slightly crunchy texture and can be substituted for rice or couscous.

Mojito Squash

Mojito is a traditional Cuban table sauce. Nick Figel, chef from the famed Cyprus Restaurant and now of the Peregrine in Highland, NC, graciously shared his talents with us one winter and introduced us to this sauce.

Sauce:

Heat olive oil in a small saucepan over medium-high heat.

Add garlic and stir, let "sizzle" for 30 seconds. Remove from heat.

Cool slightly and add lime juice, cumin, salt and pepper.

Return to stove, bring to a boil. Remove from heat. Store for 3 to 4 days in the fridge.

Slice squash lengthwise, about ½-inch thick.

Brush with sauce. Grill over hot coals until browned.

Place on serving platter and cover with remaining sauce.

Serves 4.

Try **Mojito** on any vegetables, rice, fish, chicken, or pork.

¼ cup extra virgin olive oil
3 cloves garlic, minced
6 Tbs. lime juice, fresh
¼ tsp. ground cumin
¼ tsp. salt
Black pepper to taste

3-4 medium sized yellow squash

Breads & Breakfast

Buttermilk Biscuits

Frittonis

Corn Muffins with Cheddar & Jalapeño

Nancy's Spinach Bread

Pepperoni Rolls

Focaccia with Onion & Rosemary

Gourmet Fruit Muffins

Savory Veggie Strata

Sweet Breakfast Strata

Sweet Cardamom Walnut Bread

Cranberry Orange Nut Bread

Aunt Sissy's Buttermilk Pancakes

Laurie's Cinnamon Rolls

Mushroom and Cheese Breakfast Burritos

Morgan's Breakfast

Peach Bellinis

Buttermilk Biscuits

We use this recipe for ham biscuits, a favorite hors d'oeuvre for catering events. They're also good for breakfast or with soup.

Preheat oven to 400°F.

Place flour, salt, baking powder, sugar, and soda into a large mixing bowl, blend. Cut in butter with 2 dull knives or a pastry cutter until the butter is reduced to about the size of peas. Use your hands to press butter lumps out of flour.

Make a well in the flour mixture and pour in 1⅓ cup of buttermilk. Stir with a fork adding more buttermilk if dry or more flour if too wet. Form into a ball with your hands. Knead dough a few times on a floured surface.

Roll to about ½ inch thickness. Cut biscuits into round shapes with a 2½-inch biscuit cutter or a glass.

Place on baking sheet about ½ inch apart and immediately bake for 10 to 15 minutes or until they start to brown. Remove from the oven and cool.

Makes 1 dozen large and about 2 dozen small biscuits. Store in plastic bags. This recipe doubles well.

For appetizer size biscuits, use a small fruit juice glass to cut them into 1½-inch biscuits.

Stuff biscuits with Virginia ham and serve with horseradish sauce on the side.

Horseradish sauce: ½ cup sour cream and 3 Tbs. horseradish stirred together and placed in a small bowl.

2½ cups all-purpose flour

2 tsp. salt

4 tsp. baking powder

2 tsp. sugar

1 tsp. baking soda

10 Tbs. butter, at room temperature

1⅓–1½ cups buttermilk

Frittonis

These are White Grass calzones. Thank you Rita and Tony Dannucci for this original Italian creation.

1 loaf frozen bread dough

1 jar of your favorite marinara sauce

1 cup shredded mozzarella cheese

12 oz. mushrooms, sliced

Plenty of olive oil for frying

1/4 cup Parmesan cheese

Defrost bread dough about 3 hours at room temperature on a plate sprayed with non-stick spray for easy removal. Press down dough with your fingers. Let it rise again for about 1 hour.

Cut dough into equal quarters. Roll out each into an 8-inch circle about 1/4-inch thick.

On half of each circle, place:

2 Tbs. mozzarella cheese
1 Tbs. mushrooms
1 to 2 Tbs. marinara sauce

Keep fillings away from the edge of the dough.

Moisten edge of the dough circle with water and your finger.

Fold over other half of circle and seal edge with a fork, forming a half moon shape.

Fry each Frittoni, one at a time in hot oil until golden brown on each side.

Remove to paper towel to soak up excess oil.

Serve immediately with extra sauce and Parmesan cheese.

Bread dough fried in olive oil is unbelievably good!

Makes 4.

Corn Muffins with Cheddar and Jalapeños

These muffins go great with chili!

Preheat oven to 400°F.

Sauté onion in butter until soft, and set aside.

Mix dry ingredients (cornmeal, flour, salt, cayenne, baking powder, and sugar) in a large bowl.

Whisk remaining ingredients in another bowl.

Pour wet ingredients into dry ingredients and mix until just moistened.

Spoon into greased or paper lined muffin tins and bake 25 minutes or until no longer moist in center.

Remove and cool on racks.

Makes one dozen muffins.

1	onion, minced
2	Tbs. butter
1½	cups cornmeal
½	cup flour
1	tsp. salt
	Pinch of cayenne pepper
1	Tbs. baking powder
¼	cup sugar
2	eggs
1	(8 oz.) can creamed corn
¼	cup oil
3	Tbs. minced jalapeños
1	cup grated sharp cheddar cheese
1	cup buttermilk

Nancy's Spinach Bread

Nancy Mammarella is one of our favorite bakers.
She can whip up some awesome bread in a flash.

Dough:

1	Tbs. yeast (1½ pkg.)
2	cups warm water
2	Tbs. brown sugar
1	tsp. salt
1	cup whole wheat bread flour
4	cups all-purpose flour

Filling:

1½	cups onion, chopped
3	cloves garlic, chopped
1	Tbs. olive oil
1	(10 oz.) pkg. chopped frozen spinach, thawed and squeezed
½	tsp. salt
¼	tsp. black pepper
	Pinch of red pepper flakes
1	cup ricotta cheese
½	cup mozzarella, grated
½	cup Monterey jack cheese, grated
1¼	cup Pecorino Romano cheese
½	cup Calamata olives, chopped (optional)

In a large bowl, stir yeast and sugar to dissolve. Let it sit for 5 minutes to activate. Stir in whole wheat flour and salt. Add white flour, one cup at a time, with a sturdy spoon. When most of the flour is mixed in, remove from bowl and begin kneading by hand. Work dough until smooth and elastic, adding more flour if too sticky. Knead for about 10 minutes. Clean bowl and grease. Place dough in bowl, cover with a towel and let rise for about an hour, until doubled in size.

While dough is rising, make filling by sautéing onion and garlic in olive oil for about 4 minutes over medium-high heat. Add spinach and cook 3 minutes. Add spices and remove from heat. Cool.

In a bowl, combine cheeses and chopped olives. Add spinach mixture and mix well.

Place dough on a floured surface and roll out to about 15×18 inches and ¼ inch thick.

Spread filling evenly over dough. Roll to make an 18 inch log. Place on a greased baking sheet and bring ends together to make a ring. Connect ends and pinch dough so filling will not leak out.

Bake in preheated 400°F oven for 45 minutes until bread is browned.

Let cool and slice. Serve as a sandwich or as bread with soup and salad.

Serves 6 to 10.

Pepperoni Rolls

This is a variation of Nancy's Spinach Bread, using the same dough; we've just added different fillings.

Follow directions on page 92 for dough.

Instead of spinach filling, layer pepperoni slices and cheese. Continue with directions for Nancy's Spinach Bread.

Pepperoni is just one type of filling for this sandwich. Be creative and try any or all of the following:

Prosciutto ham • smoked turkey • Virginia ham

provolone • fresh mozzarella • Swiss cheese

fresh basil leaves • fresh spinach leaves • arugula

fresh tomato slices • thin sliced onions • roasted red peppers

Lay fillings across dough, roll up and bake according to directions.

This will feed 6 to 8 as a sandwich meal.

½ pound sliced pepperoni

2 cups mozzarella or Monterey jack cheese, shredded

1 Tbs. hot pepper flakes, optional

Pepperoni rolls are a famous West Virginia food. They were invented near here in the 1920's as a portable, long lasting meal for coal miners. You'll find them in grocery stores and markets and are still a regional favorite.

Focaccia with Onions and Rosemary

Focaccia, an Italian flat bread, is traditionally hearth baked. Toppings can be varied to create unique flavors. Some bakers even make sweet focaccia with fruit and nuts.

1	pkg. dry yeast
1	cup warm water
1	tsp. sugar
½	cup whole wheat bread flour
2¾–3 cups white bread flour
2	tsp. salt
	Extra virgin olive oil
1	large onion, sliced thin
3	cloves garlic, minced
1	tsp. kosher salt
½	cup fresh grated Parmesan
1	tsp. dried rosemary

In a large bowl or the bowl of a large mixer, dissolve yeast in warm water with sugar. Set aside. When yeast mixture becomes foamy, add flour, salt and 2 Tbs. olive oil while mixing.

Once flour is incorporated, knead by hand or continue to use mixer until dough is smooth and elastic, (5 to 10 minutes). Place dough in an oiled bowl and cover with plastic wrap. Let rise until doubled in size, about one hour.

Meanwhile, heat a large skillet, add 2 Tbs. olive oil and sauté onions and garlic, cover and cook over low heat for about 30 minutes. Then uncover and increase heat to medium-high and cook until onions caramelize, about 15 minutes. Cool.

Spread dough out on an oiled baking sheet to about ½ inch thick. Press "dimples" into dough with your fingertips. Spread cooked onions over dough. Drizzle with about 3 Tbs. olive oil and sprinkle with salt, cheese and rosemary.

Bake on the top rack of a preheated 400°F oven for 25 minutes, until golden brown.

Makes about 12 slices.

Gourmet Fruit Muffins

Muffins are a brunch staple and these could become regulars for your lazy Sunday mornings. This is an adaptation of a recipe from former café baker and White Grass artist, Chris Leon Pellicoro.

Peel and grate apples in a large bowl, toss with sugar. Let sit 10 minutes.

Coarsely chop apricots and plums. Add them plus cranberries, coconut and walnuts to apples and set aside.

Preheat oven to 350°F.

In another large bowl, mix flours, soda, cinnamon and salt. Add eggs and vanilla, fold. Stir in butter then apple mixture. Do not over mix. Batter should not be smooth. Pour into lined muffin tins.

Bake for about 25 minutes, or until inserted toothpick comes out clean. Cool in pan a few minutes then remove and serve.

Makes 18 muffins.

4	cups peeled and shredded tart apples
1	cup sugar
¼	cup dried plums (about 8)
¼	cup dried apricots (about 6)
¼	cup dried cranberries
1	cup shredded unsweetened coconut
1	cup chopped walnuts
1	cup all-purpose flour
1	cup whole wheat pastry flour (see page 100)
2	tsp. baking soda
2	tsp. cinnamon
1	tsp. salt
3	large eggs, beaten
1	tsp. vanilla
¼	cup butter, melted

Savory Veggie Strata

This is a make ahead wonder. Prepare the night before and simply bake in the morning. This is very convenient for busy holiday schedules or company. Of course you can substitute other ingredients in this recipe. To satisfy meat eaters, add diced ham, cooked sausage or bacon.

1	Tbs. olive oil
1	cup onions, chopped
2	cloves garlic, minced
2	cups mushrooms, sliced
1	cup red bell pepper, diced
3/4	cup canned artichoke hearts, drained and chopped
1/4	tsp. salt
1/4	tsp. black pepper
1	loaf Italian or ciabatta bread, cubed
1/2	pound fresh spinach, washed and torn or 1 (10 oz.) frozen spinach, thawed
1	cup Asiago cheese, grated
1/2	cup cheddar cheese, grated
4	large eggs
2	cups milk

Heat a large skillet over medium-high heat. Add oil then sauté onions and garlic about 4 minutes. Add mushrooms and cook another 4 minutes. Add peppers, cook 2 minutes. Add artichokes, salt and pepper. Set aside.

Butter a 9×13-inch baking pan and line with cubed bread. Cover with spinach and cooked vegetables. Then sprinkle with cheeses.

Whisk together eggs and milk and pour over top. Cover with foil and store in refrigerator overnight (8 hours).

In the morning, remove from fridge and let set out while oven is preheating to 350°F. Bake for about an hour, until browned and bubbly.

Serves 8.

Veggie Options:

fresh sliced tomatoes • fresh basil • sautéed zucchini
black olives • shitake mushrooms
broccoli florets • asparagus • Parmesan
goat cheese • jack cheese

Use your imagination and what's in your fridge and have fun.

Sweet Breakfast Strata

This flip side strata is kind of like a pan of French toast. Add fruit (peaches, apples, raspberries or blueberries) or nuts for extra flavor.

Butter a 9×13-inch baking pan* and fill with bread cubes. Spoon ricotta cheese evenly over top.

Whisk eggs and milk and add cinnamon and syrup. Pour over bread. Cover and refrigerate overnight, (8 hours).

In the morning, remove from the fridge and let set out while oven is preheating to 350°F.

Bake for about one hour, uncovered, until brown and bubbly. Serve with butter and maple syrup.

Serves 8.

*An easy way to grease a pan is to use the waxed paper wrapper from a stick of butter. Rub the paper over the pan to prevent foods from sticking.

1	loaf cinnamon-raisin, Italian or ciabatta bread, cubed
¾	cup ricotta cheese
4	large eggs
2	cups milk
1	tsp. cinnamon
¼	cup maple syrup

We are blessed to have local baker Mimi Kibler of La Fontaine Bakery nearby. She makes incredible rustic hearth baked breads. This is not frozen dough. These are real breads, like those that you would find in Europe. We love her ciabatta and use it in many of these recipes.

Sweet Cardamom Walnut Bread

*We have served this cake with coffee for years and everyone loves it.
It's rich and sweet and worth the calories.*

1   cup butter, softened
    (2 sticks)
1   cup brown sugar
2   eggs
1   tsp. vanilla extract
1   cup all-purpose flour
1   cup whole wheat pastry
    flour (see page 100)
1   tsp. baking powder
1½ tsp. baking soda
¼   tsp. salt
1   Tbs. ground cardamom
1   cup sour cream

Filling:

2   Tbs. brown sugar
1   tsp. cinnamon
½   cup finely chopped
    walnuts

Preheat oven to 350°F. Grease a 9-inch loaf pan.

In a large mixing bowl, beat butter with sugar until light and fluffy.

Add eggs one at a time, beating well after adding each one. Stir in the vanilla.

Place dry ingredients into another bowl (not including nut mixture).

Add the flour mixture, ⅓ at a time to the butter mixture, and alternately add sour cream. Stir just enough to blend after each addition without over beating.

Combine filling ingredients in a small bowl, set aside.

Spoon half the batter into the greased loaf pan; sprinkle the nut mixture over the batter.

Spread remaining batter over the top and bake for 60 minutes or until a knife inserted all the way through comes out clean. Allow to cool in the pan for 20 minutes, run a knife around the edge and then invert onto a plate and slice.

Serves 6 to 8.

Cranberry Orange Nut Bread

Where we live, cranberries grow wild in high elevation bogs. Picking them has become an autumn tradition. We keep them in the freezer for all occasions — boy, are they tart.

Preheat oven to 350°F.

Grease one 9×5-inch loaf pan.

Combine first five ingredients in a large mixing bowl. Cut in butter to resemble coarse crumbs. Stir in berries and nuts.

Whisk together buttermilk, orange juice, orange zest, vanilla, and egg until blended. Stir into flour mixture just until moistened. Spoon batter into pan and bake for 65 minutes. Test with a toothpick for doneness. Remove from pan immediately to cool.

Serves 8 to 10.

3	cups all-purpose flour
3/4	cup sugar
2 1/2	tsp. baking powder
1/2	tsp. baking soda
1/2	tsp. salt
1/2	cup butter
1	cup fresh or frozen cranberries, coarsely chopped
1/4	cup walnuts or pecans, chopped
1/2	cup buttermilk
1/3	cup fresh orange juice
1	tsp. grated orange zest
1	tsp. vanilla
1	large egg

Zest is the peel from citrus fruit used to add tiny bits of concentrated flavor to your foods. Only use the outer peel—the inside white pith is bitter. To remove zest, use a micro plane or a small holed grater. If using a stand up grater, wrap a piece of plastic wrap over the holes to keep zest from sticking to the grater.

Aunt Sissy's Buttermilk Pancakes

Forget the box mixes, these are light and tasty and just as easy to make.

1   **cup whole wheat pastry flour**

1½ **cups all-purpose flour**

¼   **cup sugar**

2   **tsp. baking powder**

2   **tsp. baking soda**

1   **tsp. salt**

2   **cups buttermilk or soy milk**

2   **cups yogurt or sour cream**

2   **large eggs**

2   **tsp. vanilla**

    Butter for cooking

Mix together flours, sugar, powder, soda and salt.

In a separate bowl, whisk buttermilk, yogurt, eggs and vanilla. Add to dry ingredients. Stir until it just comes together, don't over mix.

Heat a griddle or large skillet. Melt a little butter and pour ⅓ cup of batter for each pancake. Cook about 3 minutes on one side. Flip and cook other side for a minute and a half. Continue to cook all pancakes, adding a little butter to the pan.

Keep warm and serve with maple syrup or one of the Sweet Sauces, see page 187.

Makes about 20 pancakes.

Whole wheat pastry flour, not to be confused with whole wheat bread flour, is a soft wheat flour with less gluten. We recommend it because it adds whole grain nutrients, better flavor and texture. If not available in your local grocery, find it at a health food store.

Laurie's Cinnamon Rolls

Using frozen bread dough speeds up the process of this recipe. By all means, make dough from scratch, if you wish. Use the recipe from Nancy's Spinach Bread, page 92.

Roll out dough on a flour covered surface to about an 8×12-inch rectangle.

Mix brown sugar, cinnamon, walnuts and raisins in a small bowl.

Dot butter over dough and sprinkle with sugar mixture.

Roll the long edge of the dough carefully into a log. Slice log into eight to ten 1-inch rounds. Place on greased baking sheet with cut side up. Cover dough with plastic wrap that has been sprayed with cooking spray, and let rise until doubled in size.*

Bake in preheated 350°F oven for 20 to 30 minutes or until slightly browned on top. Remove from oven and cool. Then glaze with the following:

Glaze

Melt butter in a small pan, add milk and stir to warm.

Stir in powdered sugar, a little at a time, to form a runny consistency. Remove from heat and drizzle over cooled rolls.

Makes 8 to 10 rolls.

*To make ahead, prepare rolls until rising stage. Store in refrigerator overnight. Remove in the morning, let rise and bake.

---

1 loaf frozen bread dough, thawed
1/8 cup brown sugar
1 tsp. cinnamon
1/4 cup walnuts
1/4 cup raisins (optional)
4 Tbs. butter, cut into bits

Glaze:

3 Tbs. butter
1/4 cup milk
1/2 cup powdered sugar

Mushroom and Cheese Breakfast Burritos

Morgan Chase, Laurie's youngest son is already a great cook, mushroom connoisseur, and especially enjoys making breakfast foods.

2	Tbs. butter
4	mushrooms sliced
1	Tbs. onions, chopped
2	eggs
1/4	cup milk
	Salt and pepper
2	flour tortillas
1/4	cup grated mozzarella or cheddar cheese

Sauté onions and mushrooms in butter in a skillet until browned.

Combine eggs, milk, salt and pepper in a bowl and whisk.

Pour egg mixture into skillet with veggies and scramble.

Divide egg into each of the tortillas and sprinkle with cheese. Roll up and serve with salsa for breakfast or any time.

Makes 2 burritos.

Morgan's Breakfast

More of Morgan's breakfast specialities.

First get a pan hot and add a little butter.

Cut a small hole in the center of the bread; place in pan.

Crack the egg into the hole, add salt and pepper.

Cook until golden brown and then flip to cook the other side.

Place fruit in a blender, then add the yogurt and juice. Blend until all the fruit is chunk-less, then enjoy.

Egg in a Nest

1   egg
1   slice of bread
    Butter
    Salt and pepper

Fruit Smoothie

1   banana, peeled and sliced
3   sliced fresh strawberries
1   cup vanilla yogurt
$\frac{1}{2}$ cup orange juice

Peach Bellinis

Thanks to Jana and Hugh Jackson for sharing this drink recipe with us.
We prepared it for them at their wedding reception brunch.

8   oz. canned peaches,
    with syrup

3   cups champagne, chilled

2   Tbs. Grand Marnier
    liquor, chilled

Process all ingredients in a blender until smooth.

Pour into champagne flutes and serve for brunch.

Serves 4 to 6.

Vegetarian Entreés

Grilled Veggie Pita with Hummus

Mary's Pinto Burgers

Anne's Spinach Casserole

Spinach Cakes

Super Sauces

Sesame Noodles

Mary's Eggplant Stir Fry

Mushroom Stroganoff

Red Beans and Rice

Baked Tofu with Snow Peas and Almonds

Summer Garden Ricotta Pie

Filo Baked Chiles Rellenos

Polenta Lasagna

Green Curry Vegetables

Butternut Mole Enchiladas

Oven Roasted Pasta Sauce

Philly Cheese Tempeh

Grilled Veggie Pita with Hummus

We've combined two great sandwiches that make one very good meal.

There are a few different ways to prepare and present this scrumptious sandwich. The vegetables can be grilled in a way best suited to you or your event. If cooking for six or more, you may want to cut veggies into chunks, brush with dressing, skewer and grill as kebabs. Present kebabs on a platter alongside hummus, lettuce, tomatoes, olives, feta cheese and warmed pita.

For a little less work, slice whole vegetables in large pieces and marinate in Italian dressing then roast or grill. Onions, peppers and portabellos should be roasted whole. Zucchini, squash and eggplant can be sliced into rounds or lengthwise in $\frac{1}{4}$-inch thick slices. Cook veggies over hot coals, about 4 minutes on each side or until lightly browned. A grill basket is another convenient way of cooking cut vegetables. Just make sure the pieces are large enough to stay in the basket.

Once vegetables are cooked, prepare sandwich. (You may want to cut veggies into smaller pieces.) Warm pita on grill a few seconds on each side, fill with hummus, then load up with veggies and toppings. Add a little more dressing and enjoy.

Serves 4.

1   zucchini

1   yellow squash

1   eggplant

12   oz. small whole white or large portabello mushrooms

1   medium sweet onion

1   red or yellow bell pepper

Italian dressing

16   oz. prepared hummus

1   pkg. pita bread

Toppings:
lettuce
grape tomatoes
olives
sprouts
feta cheese
Italian dressing

Mary's Pinto Burgers

Some of our best vegetarian recipes come from Mary Anders.

1 cup chopped onion

4 cloves garlic, minced

1 Tbs. olive oil

$\frac{1}{2}$ cup peeled and grated carrots

1 tsp. cumin

$1\frac{1}{2}$ tsp. chili powder

2 (15-oz) cans pinto or kidney beans, drained

2 Tbs. Dijon mustard

2 Tbs. soy sauce

2 Tbs. ketchup

$1\frac{1}{2}$ cups rolled oats

Salt and pepper to taste

Sauté onions and garlic in oil for about 5 minutes, until onions begin to soften. Add carrots, cumin and chili powder and cook on low heat for 5 minutes. Set aside.

Mash beans in a large bowl; add mustard, soy sauce, ketchup, and sautéed vegetables. Mix in oats. Add salt and pepper.

Moisten your hands and form the burger mixture into six 4-inch patties. Lightly oil a nonstick skillet and cook burgers on medium-low heat for 5 to 8 minutes each side.

Serve on a bun with lettuce, tomato and any of the usual burger fixings.

Makes 6 burgers.

Many of the recipes in this book start out with "saute onion and garlic in oil..." We put onions and garlic in nearly everything. Of course, everyone may not share our deep love of the bulbs. Feel free to decrease, or increase these measurements to your taste.

Anne's Spinach Casserole

Our friend, Anne Wardwell, created this low fat, gluten-free casserole.

Sauté onions in a large skillet over medium high heat until soft. Add spinach, garlic, salt and pepper and cook 5 minutes.

In a separate bowl, whisk eggs, whites, mustard and flour. Then mix in milk and cheeses.

Add spinach to egg mixture.

Pour into a greased 9×13-inch baking pan.

Bake in preheated 350°F oven for 45 minutes.

Makes 9 servings.

1	large onion, chopped
1	pound frozen chopped spinach, thawed and drained
3	cloves garlic, minced
1	tsp. salt
	Black pepper to taste
3	whole eggs
5	egg whites
1	tsp. dried mustard
6	Tbs. gluten free flour (or all-purpose flour)
2	cups skim milk
3	cups low fat cheese, Swiss and/or Pecorino Romano

Spinach Cakes

I made these as a vegetarian option for a group lunch. They immediately became a staple. This recipe makes either a great appetizer or an entrée. It all depends on how you size the patties. Try eating one on a bun with fresh tomato. MBG

2	(10 oz.) pkg. frozen chopped spinach
2	Tbs. olive oil
1	cup onion, chopped
4-6	cloves garlic, minced
1	cup mushrooms, chopped
½	cup carrots, grated
2	eggs
1	cup breadcrumbs
½	cup mayonnaise
½	tsp. salt
½	tsp. black pepper
½	tsp. dried basil
¼	tsp. dried oregano

Thaw spinach and squeeze out all water.

Heat a skillet over medium-high heat, then add oil. Wait a minute and add onions. You want them to sizzle when they hit the skillet. Cook 4 to 5 minutes or until onions start to brown. Add garlic and mushrooms and cook another 5 minutes.

In a large bowl, combine spinach, onion mixture, carrots, eggs, breadcrumbs, mayo and spices. Mix well with your hands, being sure to evenly distribute all the ingredients. Shape into patties–burger or silver dollar size.

You can cook spinach cakes one of two ways. In a skillet with a little oil until browned on each side, or in the oven on a baking sheet lightly coated with cooking spray. Bake at 375°F for 10 minutes on each side. Be sure to spray when you flip them over.

Makes 8 large or 24 appetizer sized patties. Serve with your choice of sauces from page 111 .

The size of **garlic** cloves varies. Use your judgment on how much garlic you want to add.

Super Sauces

Try one of these sauces on burgers, sandwiches, crab cakes or baked fish.

For each recipe, blend ingredients in a food processor and store in the fridge in an airtight container for up to two weeks.

Chipotle Mayo

- 1 clove garlic
- ¼ cup chopped onion
- 3 canned chipotle peppers* with adobo sauce, seeded
- 1 cup mayonnaise
- ⅓ cup sour cream
- ⅓ tsp. salt

Horseradish Mayo

- 1 cup mayonnaise
- ⅓ cup sour cream
- ¼ tsp. black pepper
- 1-1½ Tbs. prepared horseradish

Dijon Herb Sauce

- 1 cup mayonnaise
- 2 Tbs. chopped onion
- 1 clove garlic
- ¼ tsp. tarragon
- ¼ tsp. basil
- ¼ tsp. chives
- ¼ tsp. dill
- ¼ tsp. seasoned salt
-    Juice of ½ lemon
- 1 Tbs. Dijon mustard
- ¼ tsp. black pepper

*For information on chipotle peppers, see page 34.

Sesame Noodles

We make this as a vegetarian dish, but you can always add cooked chicken, beef or shrimp. Serve hot or cold and add as many veggies as you like – depending on how hungry you are.

2	Tbs. sesame seeds
1	Tbs. sesame oil
¼	cup peanut butter
2	Tbs. soy sauce
¼	cup Sweet Thai Chili sauce
¼	cup water
½	pound cooked spaghetti or soba noodles, drained
2	Tbs. fresh cilantro, chopped
2	Tbs. peanuts, chopped

Put first 6 ingredients into a blender or food processor. Blend to make sauce. Toss with hot noodles; garnish with cilantro and peanuts.

Toss in vegetables of your choice; thin sliced carrots sticks steamed snow peas, broccoli, or sweet red pepper slices

Serves 2. This recipe doubles well.

Sweet Thai Chili Sauce is a condiment we always have on hand. It's sweet, hot and garlicky. You will find many uses for it. Purchase at Asian or international groceries.

Mary's Eggplant Stir Fry

Yet another great Mary Anders recipe.

Mix the cornstarch, soy sauce and vinegar in a small bowl until smooth, set aside.

Heat 2 tablespoons of oil in a wok or large skillet. Add garlic and chilies and sauté for 30 seconds. Add 2 tablespoons oil, then add red pepper; sauté for 30 seconds. Add remaining oil and eggplant; sauté, turning often until the eggplant has softened and browned a bit, about 10 to 12 minutes.

Stir in the sauce and tofu. Cover and cook for 1 to 2 minutes. Remove from the heat and stir in cilantro. Sprinkle with sesame seeds. Serve over rice.

Serves 4.

* See information on tofu, page 50.

We've been lucky to find many talented chefs at White Grass Cafe and Mary Anders is one of them. A former civil engineer, Mary has contributed many of our vegetarian recipes. Now she travels the world but stays in touch, thanks to e-mail.

1	tsp. cornstarch
2	Tbs. soy sauce
2	Tbs. rice wine vinegar
6	Tbs. light vegetable oil
4	garlic cloves, minced
4	Serrano chilies, stemmed, seeded and minced
1	large red pepper, cut into 1-inch cubes
1	large eggplant, cut into 1-inch cubes
1	pound extra firm tofu*; drained, pressed and cut into 1-inch cubes
1/4	cup cilantro, chopped
1	Tbs. toasted sesame seeds

Mushroom Stroganoff

An elegant and simple vegetarian meal that will satisfy the hungriest crowd. If available, substitute fresh shitakes for the white mushrooms.

1	oz. dried wild mushrooms
2	Tbs. butter
1	medium onion, sliced thin, then quartered
2	cloves garlic, minced
1	Tbs. olive oil
1	pound portabello mushrooms, sliced 1/4 inch thick
1	pound fresh white mushrooms, sliced thin
1	cube vegetable bouillon or 1 Tbs. veggie broth powder
1/2	tsp. black pepper
1/2	tsp. salt
2	Tbs. soy sauce
4	Tbs. sour cream
1	tsp. Dijon mustard
1	pound egg noodles, cooked

Soak dried mushrooms in 1 cup warm water, about 20 minutes.

Meanwhile, heat a large skillet over medium-high heat for one minute. Add 1 Tbs. butter then add onion and garlic. Sauté about 5 minutes, or until lightly browned. Remove from pan. Heat pan again and add 1 Tbs. olive oil and 1 Tbs. butter. Sauté fresh mushrooms until browned, about 5 minutes.

Return onions to the pan, along with dried mushrooms. Dissolve bouillon in mushroom water and add to pan. Stir and reduce to low heat.

Add salt, pepper and soy sauce. Simmer about 10 minutes. Just before serving, stir in sour cream and Dijon.

Spoon mushrooms over prepared egg noodles.

Serves 4.

There are many varieties of **dried wild mushrooms** you can find at almost any market. Porcini, oyster, morel, chanterelle are a few good types. Their flavor is concentrated, so a few go a long way.

Red Beans & Rice

This is a vegetarian recipe but can also satisfy meat eaters by adding spicy sausage. Chorizo made with turkey or chicken is an excellent low fat choice.

Soak beans in water overnight. Drain and cook over medium heat with bay leaf and 7 cups water about 1½ hours. Pour off most of the liquid, reserve a cup for later.

Chop vegetables.

Place a large skillet over medium heat, add oil. Wait a minute and add onions, cook 3 to 4 minutes then add celery and peppers. Sauté 5 minutes. Add veggies to pot of beans. Add spices and simmer on low for 1 hour. Stir occasionally and add water or bean liquid if beans seem too thick or too dry. Adjust seasoning as needed. Serve with hot rice—Jasmine or Basmati has the best flavor.

Serves 4.

1	pound dried red beans
1	bay leaf
2	Tbs. vegetable oil
2	cups onion, chopped (one large onion)
1	cup chopped celery (about 2 stalks)
1	cup chopped red or green bell pepper
1	tsp. salt
1	tsp. black pepper
¼	tsp. cayenne pepper

If you don't have time to cook dried beans, use 2 (15 oz.) cans of red beans. Rinse and add to cooked veggies in a soup pot, then add seasoning and a little water if necessary.

Baked Tofu with Snow Peas and Almonds

½ cup whole almonds

1 pound extra-firm tofu*; drained, pressed and cut into 1-inch cubes

1½ Tbs. sesame oil

2 Tbs. soy sauce

½ cup whole almonds

2 cups snow peas

Thinly sliced scallions for garnish

Dressing:

1½ Tbs. vegetable oil

2 tsp. sesame oil

2 Tbs. rice vinegar

2 tsp. grated fresh ginger

½ tsp. coriander

1 tsp. brown sugar

¼ tsp. salt

Place almonds in a baking sheet and toast in a 350°F oven for 5 minutes.

Arrange tofu in a single layer on a baking sheet.

Mix soy sauce and sesame oil together and pour over the tofu. Bake for 30 minutes at 350°F. Turn tofu so that all surfaces get brown and crispy. Let cool.

Blanch snow peas in boiling water for 3 minutes, drain.

Combine dressing ingredients and toss with tofu, snow peas and almonds. Garnish with scallions and serve immediately with hot rice or noodles.

Serves 2 to 3.

*For information on tofu, see page 50.

Summer Garden Ricotta Pie

Raid the garden, or stock up at the Farmer's Market for the goodies that will make this luscious, light supper. For a quicker fix, use refrigerated pie crust.

Prepare and bake pie crust according to directions, cool.

Chop onions and sauté in ½ Tbs. of olive oil until golden brown, about 5 minutes. Cool slightly.

In a food processor, blend basil and parsley with 1 Tbs. olive oil. Add salt and pepper. Then add onions and olives and pulse 3 to 4 times.

In a mixing bowl, blend ricotta, eggs and cheese. Gently mix well. Fold in basil mixture and pour into pie shell. Arrange sliced tomatoes on top.

Bake in preheated 400°F oven for 45 minutes, or until golden on top. Remove from oven and cool at least 15 minutes before serving.

Serves 4 as an entrée or 6 to 8 as a side dish.

1	(9-inch) pastry pie shell, see page 182.
1	cup chopped onions
1½	Tbs. extra virgin olive oil
1½	cups fresh basil leaves
1	cup fresh parsley leaves
¼	tsp. salt
½	tsp. black pepper
⅓	cup Calamata olives
2	cups ricotta cheese
3	eggs, beaten
½	cup Parmigiano-Reggiano cheese, grated
1-2	tomatoes, thinly sliced

Filo Baked Chiles Rellenos

*Not exactly the traditional way to make chiles rellenos,
but a little easier and very delicious.*

6	whole poblano peppers*
1	medium onion, chopped
2	Tbs. oil
2	cloves garlic, minced
8	oz. Monterey jack cheese, grated
1/2	pound filo dough, thawed
1	stick butter, melted
6	eggs, beaten
1/4	tsp. salt
1/2	tsp. ground cumin

Cook whole peppers over a hot grill, or under an oven broiler until charred on all sides. Let cool then remove black skin and slice peppers into wide strips.

In the meantime, heat a skillet over medium high heat and sauté onions and garlic until soft, about 5 minutes.

Unwrap filo and gently drape two sheets over a 9×13-inch pan. Brush filo with butter, place another two layers and butter. Continue until you have 8 layers of filo. Lay sliced peppers in pan and cover with grated cheese.

In a small bowl, whisk eggs and add spices. Pour over peppers.

Continue to layer filo, 2 sheets at a time, remembering to brush with melted butter until you have 8 sheets of dough. Tuck overhanging dough inside the edges of the pan. Bake in preheated 375°F oven for 35 minutes. Let cool about 10 minutes before serving.

Serves 4 to 6.

*An easier way is to use chopped canned green chiles. You can skip the pepper roasting sequence and jump straight into the onions.

Working with filo can be challenging. Make sure you thaw it in the fridge at least a day before using. If you have it out for more than ten minutes, cover it with a clean damp towel to prevent it from drying out.

Polenta Lasagna

This recipe is similar to vegetable lasagna but uses polenta instead of noodles.

Make the polenta at least 1½ hours or the night before you prepare the lasagna.

Boil 4 cups of water and gradually whisk in the cornmeal. Reduce heat to medium. Stir constantly until the polenta is thick, about 10 minutes. Season with rosemary and salt and pepper.

Pour polenta about ¾ inches thick into two 8×8-inch pans (to make two layers). Spread evenly into pans and chill for one hour or until firm.

Preheat oven to 400°F. To roast the eggplant, prick it with a fork and place it on a baking sheet and bake for 45 minutes or until flesh is soft. Scoop out the soft inside, discarding the skin, and chop coarsely. Reduce oven to 350°F.

Sauté the red pepper, mushrooms, kale, onion, and garlic in oil for 5 to 8 minutes. Transfer to a bowl and add eggplant, basil, oregano, and beans. Stir to blend.

Remove polenta onto wax paper. Pour 1 cup of marinara into one of the 8×8-inch pans and spread on the bottom. Place one layer of polenta on top of the marinara sauce. Add all the vegetable filling on top of the polenta. Top with mozzarella. Put on the second layer of polenta and top with more marinara and Parmesan. Cover and bake at 350°F for 30 minutes or until the dish is heated through. Let lasagna stand for 10 minutes before serving.

Serves 4.

Polenta:

4 cups water

1½ cups cornmeal

¼ tsp. fresh rosemary

Salt and pepper to taste

Vegetable Filling:

1 eggplant

1 Tbs. olive oil

1 sweet red pepper, chopped

2 cups mushrooms, diced

½ bunch fresh kale, chopped

1 cup onion, chopped

2 cloves garlic, minced

2 Tbs. fresh basil, minced

2 Tbs. fresh oregano, minced

½ cup cannelloni beans

¼ cup mozzarella cheese

3 cups marinara sauce

¼ cup Parmesan cheese

Green Curry Vegetables

This is simply a Thai stir-fry. The only musts here are the curry paste and coconut milk. Otherwise, use any vegetables you wish. Chicken or shrimp can also be added for meat eaters.

2	Tbs. vegetable oil, preferably peanut
3	cups cabbage, sliced thin
1	large onion, chopped
2	cups butternut squash, peeled and diced into 1-inch cubes
1	red bell pepper, sliced into strips
3	cups broccoli crowns and chopped stems
3	carrots, sliced diagonally
½	pound greens (spinach, kale or swiss chard)
1	cup fresh corn kernels
2	Tbs. Thai green curry paste
2	(14 oz.) cans coconut milk
2	cups basmati rice

Chop all vegetables, keep separate.

Heat a wok over medium-high heat. Then add oil. Cook vegetables, one at a time, in order listed, starting with cabbage. Sauté for about 2 to 3 minutes. Push cooked veggies to the sides of the wok and add new ones to the center. Continue until all veggies are added.

Stir in curry paste and coconut milk. Simmer about 7 minutes.

Steam or boil rice according to package directions. Spoon veggies over rice.

Serves 6.

If you don't have a wok, use your largest skillet. Cook vegetables one at a time then add to a large soup pot. Simmer in pot until serving.

* Thai Green Curry paste can be purchased at an Asian market or a specialty food section of a large grocery store.

Optional ingredients:
tofu • mushrooms • asparagus • green beans • snow peas
water chestnuts • bok choy • cauliflower florets • celery
frozen peas • squash • zucchini

Butternut Mole Enchiladas with Tomatillo Salsa

This is an excellent vegetarian version of a classic Mexican dish inspired by our friend and the graphic designer of this book, Lisa Bridges.

Peel squash, remove seeds and using a large strong knife, cut into 1-inch cubes. (Winter squashes are dense, so take care when cutting them).

In a large skillet, heat oil, then add onion and garlic. Sauté until lightly browned, about 5 minutes. Stir in mole and add ¾ cup water, mix until mole is dissolved. Add squash, salt, and pepper and more water if needed. Simmer on low for 20 to 30 minutes. Squash should be swimming in a medium-thick sauce.

Warm corn tortillas in a dry skillet. Spoon squash into tortilla, cover with cheese and immediately serve with salsa, rice and Black Bean and Sweet Potato Chili, page 34.

Serves 4.

Tomatillo Salsa

Peel papery skins off tomatillos and rinse. In a large, heavy skillet, brown tomatillos lightly on all sides over medium high heat. Then cool.

Meanwhile, pulse onion, garlic, and jalapeño in a food processor until coarsely chopped. Then add tomatillos, cilantro, salt, pepper and lime. Pulse until mixture is just a little chunky. Store in fridge until serving.

* Mole paste is a Mexican condiment you can purchase in the Hispanic section of most groceries.

1	large butternut squash
1	Tbs. olive oil
1	medium onion, chopped
3	cloves garlic
¼	cup mole paste*
1	tsp. salt
½	tsp. black pepper
1	dozen corn tortillas
2	cups Monterey jack cheese, grated

Tomatillo Salsa

1½	pounds tomatillos
½	medium onion
2	cloves garlic
1	small fresh jalapeño pepper, seeded
½	cup fresh cilantro
½	tsp. salt
½	tsp. black pepper
	Juice of ½ lime

Oven Roasted Pasta Sauce

Charlie Waters is a great gardener and cook (amongst many other things). End of summer is harvest time — there's lots to do. She makes panfuls of this sauce and cans it to enjoy all winter.

1 medium eggplant
1 medium onion
3 cloves garlic
8 tomatoes
1 bell pepper
¼ cup extra virgin olive oil
 Salt and pepper
 Fresh basil leaves
 Oregano

Peel and cut eggplant into 1-inch cubes.

Cut tomatoes in half and gently squeeze out seeds.

Slice peppers into thin strips, then in half.

Chop onion into ½-inch chunks.

Slice garlic into thin pieces.

Toss all veggies with olive oil. Sprinkle with salt and pepper.

Place on a baking sheet. Make sure tomatoes are laying cut side down.

Roast in a preheated 350°F oven for about an hour. They will become mushy.

Remove from oven, pull skins off tomatoes. Spoon and scrape everything from pan into a large pot. Add desired amount of basil and oregano, stir well with a sturdy spoon.

Serve right away or keep for several days. This will freeze well for later use.

Serve over your favorite pasta or as a topping for pizza or a filling for lasagna.

Serves 6.

Philly Cheese Tempeh

Similar to the famous steak sandwich, this vegetarian version is hearty and very tasty. This recipe makes three large sandwiches.

Slice tempeh into wide strips then halve lengthwise and sprinkle with seasoned salt.

Heat a large skillet over medium heat. Add 1 Tbs. oil and cook tempeh until brown on both sides. (You may have to add a little more oil). Remove tempeh and set aside.

Add 2 Tbs. oil, increase heat to medium-high and sauté onion and peppers 5 minutes or until lightly browned. Remove from heat and add tempeh to skillet. Cover and let set a few minutes.

Warm rolls; spread with mayo. Fill with hot tempeh and peppers. Cover with sliced cheese and smush it all together and take a big bite. Enjoy.

Makes 3 sandwiches.

1	(8 oz.) pkg. tempeh
1/2	tsp. seasoned salt
3	Tbs. olive oil
1	medium onion, thinly sliced
1/2	red bell pepper, thinly sliced
1/2	yellow or green bell pepper, thinly sliced
3	French or hoagie rolls
1/2	pound sliced provolone or jack cheese
	Mayonnaise

Tempeh is a meat substitute made from soybeans that are fermented and shaped into cakes. Sometimes rice or other beans are added. It has a firm, chewy texture and works well grilled or skillet browned. Purchase in the refrigerated section of a health food store.

Meats

Chaing Mai Chicken

Scott's Chicken and Cabbage

Cajun Chicken Pasta

Enchiladas Suizas

Grilled Chicken Tex Mex Wrap

Grilled Chicken Shish Kebab

Turkey Pot Pie

Quick Turkey Tacos

Pizza Party

Green Chile Pork Enchiladas

Pork Tenderloin Cilantro Pesto

Slow Cooked Pulled Pork

Burgundy Beef Tenderloin

Appalachian Pot Roast

Venison Hash (Stew)

Thai Venison Roast

Chaing Mai Chicken

Former café staffer Melanie Hall gave us this very easy, very spicy dish.

Bring water to a boil in a large pot.

Add salt, and chicken and simmer on medium heat, about 20 minutes. Remove chicken and cool. Reserve broth. Cut meat into bite sized pieces; set aside.

In a large saucepan, heat coconut milk, broth, curry paste, turmeric, fish sauce, soy sauce, lime juice and seasonings. Stir to dissolve the curry paste.

When well heated, add chicken and vegetables. Serve with hot rice.

Serves 4.

2	quarts water
1	pound boneless, skinless, chicken breasts or thighs
1/2	tsp. salt
2 1/2	cups coconut milk
2 1/2	cups chicken broth
1-2	Tbs. red curry paste
1	tsp. turmeric
4	Tbs. fish sauce
1	Tbs. soy sauce
	Juice of 1/2 lime
	Salt and pepper to taste
1	bunch broccoli, steamed and cut into bite sized pieces
1	can bamboo shoots, drained
	(Optional vegetable additions: steamed carrot sticks, snow peas or zucchini sticks)

Scott's Chicken and Cabbage

Long time White Grasser and one of our favorite cooks, Scott Weaner, gave us this Thai recipe. You will need to go to an Asian market to find some of the ingredients.

1	Tbs. red curry paste
1	Tbs. fish sauce
1	tsp. sugar (Scott uses raw sugar)
1	Tbs. lime juice
8	peppercorns
1	tsp. cilantro root or 2 Tbs. chopped fresh cilantro
1/4	tsp. salt
3	chicken breasts, boned and sliced into 2-inch pieces
3	cups coconut milk
1/2	tsp. Laos powder or galangal*
3	cups coarsely chopped cabbage

Mix together curry paste, fish sauce, sugar and lime juice. Set aside until just before serving.

Combine peppercorns, cilantro root and salt. Mash into a paste; a mortar and pestle work well.

Put cilantro paste in wok with chicken, coconut milk and Laos powder, or galangal. Cook over medium heat and bring to a boil. Continue cooking until chicken is just tender. Add cabbage and boil until cooked, but still crisp. Serve with rice and sprinkle with sauce.

Serves 4.

* If not available, substitute with ½ tsp. fresh grated ginger and ⅛ tsp. black pepper.

Cajun Chicken Pasta

Nothing is better after a day of skiing than this velvety dish. Our friend and local innkeeper Susan Moore graciously gave us this recipe.

Dice chicken into 1-inch cubes, and sprinkle with seasonings, set aside. (Chicken is easier to cut when partially frozen).

Heat a large skillet over medium-high heat, add oil and cook chicken until browned, about 5 minutes. Remove chicken from pan; leave juices.

Add onions to pan and sauté 2 to 3 minutes. Add peppers and cook until soft, about 5 minutes. Stir in tomatoes and their juices. Simmer about 30 minutes.

Then add chicken, stir well. Cover and simmer on low until liquid reduces to about half, about 20 minutes.

In the meantime, cook pasta and drain. Just before serving, stir cream and parsley into the chicken. Spoon chicken over individual plates of pasta.

Serves 4.

$1\frac{1}{2}$ pounds boneless, skinless chicken thighs

1 tsp. salt

1 tsp. black pepper

$\frac{1}{4}$ tsp. cayenne pepper

Pinch of thyme

Pinch of celery seed

1 Tbs. vegetable oil

1 medium onion, chopped (1 cup)

1 red bell pepper, chopped (1 cup)

1 (16 oz.) can diced tomatoes

$\frac{1}{4}$ cup fresh parsley, chopped

1 pint heavy cream

1 pound fettuccini noodles

Enchiladas Suizas

Believe it or not, a vegetarian gave us this recipe.
Thanks Mary!

2 cups cooked chicken, chopped or shredded

1 small can green chiles

1 (7 oz.) can green chile salsa (salsa verde)

½ tsp. salt

2 cups heavy whipping cream

12 corn tortillas

Oil for frying

1½ cups shredded Monterey jack cheese

Combine chicken, chiles and salsa for filling.

Mix salt and cream in a pie plate.

Fry each tortilla for a few seconds in 2 Tbs. oil, until it blisters and is limp. Dip tortilla in cream, fill with chicken mixture, roll up, and place in ungreased baking dish.

Pour remaining cream over enchiladas and sprinkle with cheese. Bake, uncovered, at 350°F for 15 to 20 minutes. Serves 6.

This goes well with Cilantro Rice, page 81 or Black Bean and Sweet Potato Chili, page 34.

Grilled Chicken Tex-Mex Wrap

This recipe is slightly more involved than a quick PB&J. Make it for a special occasion brunch or dinner.

Mix oil, cumin and lime juice and marinate chicken for 30 minutes.* Then prepare a grill.

In a skillet, over medium-high heat, sauté onions and garlic in a little oil until browned. Cool and mix in a bowl with grated cheese, set aside.

Place peppers on hot grill, turning until blackened on all sides. Remove and cool; then peel off charred skins.

Make a slit and remove seeds. Stuff each pepper with the cheese/onion mixture and place on a baking sheet. Set aside.

Grill chicken 5 to 7 minutes on each side, depending on the thickness of the meat. Remove from grill and slice into strips.

Place stuffed peppers in a 350°F oven for 15 minutes. Meanwhile, heat flour tortillas on grill. Fill each tortilla with chicken strips and one stuffed pepper. Serve with salsa mixed with fresh chopped cilantro.

Serves 6.

*If you want a garlicky flavor, you can use the Mojito sauce as a marinade, see page 85.

3	Tbs. vegetable oil
1/4	tsp. ground cumin
	Juice of one lime
1	pound boneless, skinless chicken breasts
1/2	medium onion, chopped
2	cloves garlic, minced
1	Tbs. oil
8	oz. Montèrey jack cheese, grated
6	whole poblano peppers
6	flour tortillas
	Tomato salsa
	Fresh cilantro

Grilled Chicken Shish Kebab

Another delicious recipe from Scott Weaner. He travels the world and brings back amazing recipes—thanks.

2 pounds boneless, skinless chicken breasts

1 cup yogurt

1/3 cup virgin olive oil

2 Tbs. lemon juice

3 cloves garlic, minced

1 tsp. paprika

1/4 tsp. salt

1/4 tsp. freshly ground black pepper

Yogurt Garlic Sauce

1 2/3 cups yogurt

4 cloves garlic, minced

Salt to taste

1/2 tsp. extra virgin olive oil

2 Tbs. fresh parsley, chopped

Cut chicken into 1-inch cubes.

Mix yogurt, olive oil, lemon juice, garlic, paprika, salt and pepper in a bowl and add chicken. Refrigerate at least 30 minutes and up to 2 hours. Stir once or twice while marinating.

Prepare a grill.

Place chicken on skewers. Grill over hot coals, about 8 minutes, turning often and basting with leftover marinade.

Option: Add chunks of onion, peppers and cherry tomatoes to skewers.

Mix ingredients for yogurt sauce in a small bowl. Spoon sauce over shish kebab. Serve on pita bread with rice.

Serves 4.

Turkey Pot Pie

This is a great way to use up Thanksgiving leftovers.

Cut potatoes, cover with water add ½ tsp. salt and boil in a saucepan, 15 to 20 minutes, or until tender, drain.

Meanwhile, sauté onion and garlic in oil for 4 minutes. Add celery, carrots, salt, rosemary and pepper. Cook about 5 minutes.

In a 9×13-inch baking dish, layer turkey, onion mixture, potatoes and peas, set aside.

Sauce:

In a medium skillet, heat butter and stir in flour, blend. Add milk and whisk until smooth. Then add warm broth and whisk, cook over medium-low heat about 5 minutes.

Pour sauce over vegetables and turkey. Gently mix.

Unroll puff pastry and cover filling. Bake in preheated 400° oven for 45 minutes.

Serves 6 to 8 generously.

*Rather than using very salty canned broth, we make our own broth by boiling cooked turkey bones in 3 cups water. If you choose to use canned, omit the 1 tsp. salt in this recipe.

2	medium potatoes, cubed
½	tsp. salt
½	Tbs. vegetable oil
1½	cups onion, chopped
1	clove garlic, minced
⅔	cup celery, chopped
1	cup carrots, diced
1	tsp. salt
¼	tsp. dried rosemary, crushed
½	tsp. black pepper
4	cups cooked turkey, diced
1	(10 oz.) pkg. frozen peas
1	pkg. frozen puff pastry, thawed

Sauce:

3	Tbs. butter
½	cup flour
1¼	cup milk
2	cups broth*

Quick Turkey Tacos

Prepare this for a quick supper. Ground turkey is lighter tasting and has less fat than ground beef.

1	Tbs. olive oil
1	medium onion, chopped
1	medium green pepper, chopped
1	banana wax pepper, chopped
3	cloves garlic, minced
1	pound ground turkey
1	Tbs. chili powder
1	tsp. cumin
2	tsp. Goya Adobo seasoning or seasoned salt
	Flour tortillas, warmed

Sauté onion, peppers, and garlic in oil. Add the ground turkey and continue to cook.

Season with spices and stir well. Simmer until turkey is well done. Serve rolled in flour tortillas with suggested toppings.

This seasoned turkey also makes a great taco salad topping.

Refried beans and rice go well with this meal.

Serves 4.

Suggested toppings:

lettuce • fresh tomato • guacamole

grated Monterey jack cheese • salsa • sour cream

fresh chopped cilantro

Goya Adobo All Purpose Seasoning is my new favorite seasoning. I use it in just about everything; fried eggs, soups, meats, and fish. LKL

Pizza Party

This is a great theme dinner for a crowd and really fun for kids. Keep a camera handy because you may want to photograph some of the beautiful designs people will make.

The recipe is simple – lay out a big selection of your favorite pizza toppings. Give each person a flour tortilla and let them build their own dinner. You may need to do some prep work, but that can be done ahead of time. Make it as easy or complicated as you have time for. Cook pizzas in shifts for 5 to 10 minutes at 450°F.

Here are some ideas for toppings:

Pizza sauce

Sliced mushrooms

Sautéed onions

Sliced red and green peppers

Cheeses – feta, mozzarella, jack

Fresh spinach

Peeled cooked shrimp

Pineapple chunks

Artichoke hearts

Red pepper flakes

Broccoli florets

Sliced cooked chicken

Thai peanut sauce

Olives

Pepperoni or bacon

Sausage

Toasted pine nuts

Goat cheese

Dried cranberries

Sautéed zucchini and squash

Fresh basil

Pesto

Cherry tomatoes

Ricotta cheese

Sliced avocados

Asparagus

Fresh or roasted garlic

Tapenade (page 19)

Anchovies

Green Chile Pork Enchiladas

For an easier dinner, cook the meat ahead, a day or two, and assemble enchiladas just before eating. The flavors will blend and become better with a little time.

4-5 pound pork butt or shoulder

Salt and pepper

1 Tbs. vegetable oil

1 large onion, chopped

4 cloves garlic, minced

⅓ cup mole paste (available in Hispanic section at grocery)

2 (6oz.) cans green chiles

½ tsp. salt

1 pkg. corn tortillas

8 oz. grated Monterey jack cheese

Rinse meat and trim off any excess fat and sprinkle with salt and pepper. Place in a dutch oven or other oven roaster with a tight fitting lid. Slowly bake at 300°F for 5 to 6 hours. When ready, meat will flake apart with a fork. Let meat cool in pan. Skim off any fat and leave juices.

In a large skillet, heat oil, then add onions and garlic. Sauté 5 to 8 minutes or until browned. Stir in mole and slowly add 1 cup water. Reduce heat to low and simmer. Meanwhile, flake pork into bite-sized pieces and add with juices to mole. Add more water if needed. Pork should be swimming in a thick sauce. If necessary, add more mole. Stir in green chiles and salt. Time on the stove will not hurt this recipe. Simmer up to an hour for best results.

When ready to serve, heat a skillet on the stove and warm tortillas 1 minute on each side. Heat all tortillas. Place one flat on a plate and spoon on meat. Sprinkle with a little cheese. Place another tortilla on top with just a little meat and sauce to moisten and add more cheese. Ideally, it is best to then broil the plate so the cheese browns on top, but not necessary. Serve with spicy black beans and rice on the side.

Enough for 6 generous portions.

Pork Tenderloin Stuffed with Cilantro Lime Pesto

Try this for a different southwest supper.

Preheat oven to 400°F.

Cut tenderloin lengthwise almost in half. Open and lay flat between two sheets of wax paper. Pound with a meat mallet or rolling pin to ½-inch thickness.

Place garlic, onion, cilantro, lime juice and jalapenos into food processor or blender. Process until coarsely chopped. Continue processing while slowly adding oil until mixture is slightly smooth.

Spread half the pesto mixture over tenderloin; top with cheese. Roll up and secure meat with string. Spread remaining pesto mixture over the top of the meat. Place on rack in roasting pan.

Bake for 20 to 25 minutes or until an instant read thermometer reads 170°F in the middle of the meat. Cool 5 minutes and then remove string. Slice and serve with Picante sauce.

Serves 6.

1 ½ pound pork tenderloin

3 cloves garlic, minced

¼ cup chopped onion

½ cup loosely packed chopped fresh cilantro

2 Tbs. fresh lime juice

1 tsp. jalapeno, diced

2 Tbs. olive oil

½ cup shredded Monterey jack cheese

Green chile picante sauce

Slow Cooked Pulled Pork

This is a great way to feed a crowd with little effort. You can even cook the meat overnight. It can cook for 8 hours if you lower the temperature to 275°F.

2	Tbs. cumin seed
2	Tbs. brown sugar
¼	cup paprika
2	Tbs. chili powder
1	Tbs. ground red pepper
2	Tbs. salt
2	Tbs. cracked black pepper
1	(5 pound) pork butt or shoulder
1-2	cups prepared barbeque sauce

Make a dry rub by toasting cumin seed in a dry pan over medium high heat. Stir and remove from heat when it starts to become fragrant. Avoid burning. Add brown sugar, paprika, chili powder, red pepper, salt and pepper, mix together. Store in a sealed jar.

Preheat oven to 300°F.

Season meat with as much dry rub to coat all sides. Place in a baking pan not much larger than the meat requires and cover with foil. Bake in a slow oven for 5 to 6 hours or until pork pulls easily into chunks.

Tear or cut into shreds; remove any fat. Then mix with your favorite barbeque sauce. Serve hot with buns and cole slaw.

Serves 8 to 10.

Burgundy Beef Tenderloin

This is a special occasion kind of entrée and is perfectly complimented with flavored mashed potatoes and oven roasted asparagus.

Trim beef of fat.

Make marinade by whisking red wine, vinegar, rosemary, salt, pepper and olive oil.

Place beef in a tight fitting pan.

Prick meat all over with a fork and pour on marinade. Turn to coat. Cover with foil.

Refrigerate for 2 to 24 hours.

Heat oven to 425°F.

Roast meat about 25 to 45 minutes, until an instant read thermometer reaches:

> 120°F for rare
>
> 125°F to 130°F for medium rare
>
> 135°F to 140°F for medium

Remember that the temperature will continue to rise 5 to 10 degrees out of oven.

Remove to platter and cover with foil loosely and let stand 10 to 20 minutes before carving.

In a saucepan, cook mushrooms and garlic 3 minutes in butter, then add juices from the baking pan. Cook for 15 to 20 minutes.

Slice beef into ½-inch thick slices and arrange on a rimmed platter. Taste and adjust salt and pepper.

Pour sauce over beef just before serving.

Makes 10 to 12 servings.

1	(5 pound) beef tenderloin
½	cup dry red wine
4	Tbs. balsamic vinegar
2	tsp. dried rosemary
1½	tsp. black pepper
2	tsp. salt
¼	cup olive oil
1½	pounds mushrooms, sliced in half
1½	Tbs. garlic, minced
1	Tbs. butter

Appalachian Pot Roast with Ramps

Every April we look forward to the arrival of ramps. The wild leeks that grow all over the Appalachian hills are a pungent harbinger of spring and a healthful tonic, too.

5-6 pounds of boneless chuck roast

1 tsp. seasoned salt

$\frac{1}{2}$ tsp. black pepper

4-6 small red potatoes

1 pound medium carrots, peeled and cut in half

1 medium onion, quartered

2 handfuls of cleaned ramps with green leaves

This is not a complicated dish but the key to a tender pot roast is slow cooking, so you can't be in a hurry for this meal. Rinse the meat and trim off any excess fat. Lightly dust with seasoned salt and pepper. Place in a large heavy dutch oven or any oven roasting pan with a tight fitting lid and put in a 275°F preheated oven. Let the meat bake for about 4 hours. Then add potatoes, carrots and onion and put back in the oven for another 45 minutes. Add ramps, cover again and bake another 20 minutes or until ramps are wilted and tender. Remove from oven and let rest about 10 minutes. Beef should easily come apart with a fork.

Serves 4 to 6.

The **ramp or wild leek** resembles a scallion with two wide leaves. They pop up just as the snow leaves. Considered a spring delicacy in West Virginia, the ramp is honored at many festivals and town dinners. They are added in the place of onions in many dishes; fried with potatoes, steamed, pickled and baked. Since they are only around for a short time, people like to indulge. After eating ramps, their distinct pungent flavor will permeate your body and you will begin to smell like one. No one will notice if you hang out with other ramp lovers.

Venison Hash (Stew)

Ruth Melnick organizes our "ski hash" events and makes this delicious stew every time. The hash is a ski chase through the woods where a pack of skiers (hounds) try to catch the "hares" that set the course. It's a drinking club with a skiing problem. Lots of fun.

Combine Jerk paste and olive oil and rub into venison meat. Allow to marinate refrigerated for a couple of hours (or longer). Dry roast meat in a covered roasting pan at 325°F for about 1 hour or until cooked to medium. Or roast on a charcoal grill using indirect heat for about half an hour. Allow to cool and then cut into 1-inch cubes.

In a heavy bottomed stew pot, cook minced bacon over medium heat until cooked but not crispy. Add butter, crushed bay leaf, basil, celery, carrots, onion, and garlic. Cook until soft then mash slightly.

Now add flour and allow to fatten, stirring constantly (about 5 minutes). Add tomato sauce stirring constantly (base will thicken quite a bit at this point, so keep it moving). Next add beef broth and use a whisk to whip out lumps. (You can pour the base through a strainer to catch and mash up lumps.) Add peppercorns and sherry and simmer for 15 to 20 minutes.

Add potatoes and allow to simmer for 15 min.

Add mushrooms and simmer another 15 min.

Add cubed venison and parsley and simmer until meat is fully reheated.

Salt and pepper to taste. Garnish with a little parsley and enjoy.

NOTE: If you want it to be a little spicier, add more jerk paste a half teaspoon at a time (it will get spicier as it sets.)

1	(2-2½) pound venison tenderloin or leg (you can substitute beef)
2	Tbs. olive oil
3	Tbs. Jamaican jerk paste
4	strips bacon, minced
3	Tbs. butter
1	bay leaf, crushed
1	tsp. dry basil
2	stalks celery, minced
2	carrots, minced
1	small onion, minced
2	cloves garlic, minced
¼	cup flour
4	cups tomato sauce
6	cups beef broth
1	tsp. black peppercorns
½	cup dry sherry
5	medium potatoes peeled and cut into 1 inch cubes
1	pound sliced mushrooms
1	cup parsley, chopped

Thai Venison Roast

Every Jack Frost (our annual White Grass welcome-to-winter celebration) Jeff and Ruth Melnick grill a venison quarter. It has been a tasty tradition.

1	(5) pound venison roast (or beef)
1	can coconut milk (14 oz.)
4	Tbs. masaman curry paste

Combine coconut milk and curry. Marinate roast in a plastic bag, refrigerated, at least 2 hours or overnight.

Prepare coals or heat a gas grill. Place coals to one side of the grill. Place meat on opposite side, not above coals. This is an indirect cooking method.

Roast meat for about 45 minutes or until an instant read thermometer reaches 140°F. Remove from heat and let rest for about 20 minutes before slicing.

Fish

Spaghetti Squash with Smoked Salmon

Sesame Salmon Cakes

Salmon with Honey Lime Ginger Sauce

Trout Baked with Dijon Herb Sauce

Trout in Champagne Cream Sauce

Whole Stuffed Grilled Trout

Crab and Shrimp Lasagna

Dave's Shrimp Risotto

Indonesian Grilled Shrimp

Sea Scallops in Saffron Cream

Steamed Mussels in White Wine

Grilled Tuna with Herb Shallot Marinade

Bombay Chutney for Fish

Sweet Wild Leek (Ramp) Sauce for Fish

Teriyaki Sauce for Fish

Spaghetti Squash with Smoked Salmon

This is one of the easiest recipes in this book. But that doesn't mean you can't serve it at a fancy dinner party.

Slice squash in half lengthwise and scoop out seeds. Place cut side down on a baking sheet and place in a preheated 350°F oven. Add 1 to 2 cups water to pan and bake for 45 to 55 minutes, until squash is tender when stuck with a fork. Remove from oven and cool, about 5 minutes.

Lightly scrape into strands, using a fork. Squash will flake apart, like spaghetti.

Place in a bowl and toss with butter, Parmesan and a little salt and pepper.

Sprinkle flaked fish over top of squash and serve.

Serves 4.

1	spaghetti squash (appx. 2 pounds)
2	Tbs. butter
1/4	cup Parmesan cheese
5	oz. hot smoked salmon or trout
	Salt and pepper to taste
	Red pepper flakes (optional)

Cold smoked fish, like lox, is smoked at a lower temperature and is raw. Hot smoked fish is smoked at a high enough temperature to actually cook the fish and has more of a salty and sweet smoky flavor. It can be eaten without any further cooking.

Sesame Salmon Cakes

We've given this salmon an Asian flair. This is a great use for leftover salmon.

1½ pounds fresh salmon

2 cloves garlic, minced

4 green onions, chopped

¼ cup onion, minced

½ cup cilantro, minced

1 Tbs. fresh ginger root, grated

3 Tbs. soy sauce

½ tsp. sesame seeds

½ cup mayonnaise

1 egg

1 tsp. toasted sesame oil

1 cup breadcrumbs

½ tsp. black pepper

Cook salmon on a foil lined baking sheet at 350°F for 12 to 15 minutes, then set aside to cool.

Meanwhile, chop veggies by hand or pulse in a food processor. Mix in a large bowl with soy sauce, sesame seeds, mayo, egg and sesame oil.

Flake fish into bowl and add breadcrumbs and pepper. Mix well, using your hands for best blending.

Shape into patties. You can cook them now or keep in fridge for a day. They can also be frozen at this stage for later use.

To serve, brown in a skillet with a small amount of oil. Cook about 3 minutes on each side over medium heat.

Makes 8 patties.

For a delicious appetizer, shape into golf ball sized patties. Brown and serve with dipping sauce on page 15.

Salmon with Honey Lime Ginger Sauce

This quick-to-make sauce creates a sweet and tangy flavor and keeps the fish from drying out. Serve with lots of sautéed fresh vegetables.

Preheat oven to 375°F.

Rinse fillets and place on a foil lined baking sheet.

In a small saucepan, melt butter over medium heat and add garlic, sauté 1 to 2 minutes. Stir in honey, ginger and lime juice until well mixed.

Pour sauce over salmon and bake about 10 to 15 minutes. Cooking time will vary depending on thickness of fish. Do not over cook fish.

Serves 4.

$1\frac{1}{2}$ pounds fresh salmon fillets (up to 1 inch thick)

$\frac{1}{2}$ Tbs. butter

1 clove garlic, minced

$\frac{1}{2}$ cup honey

$\frac{1}{2}$ tsp. fresh ginger root, grated

Juice of one lime

Trout Baked with Dijon Herb Sauce

This is a perfect sauce for a delicate fish like trout.
It also works well with any mild white fish.

1	cup mayonnaise
2	Tbs. chopped onion
1	clove garlic
1/4	tsp. dried tarragon
1/4	tsp. dried basil
	Pinch of dill weed
1/2	tsp. Old Bay seasoning
	Juice of 1 lemon
1	Tbs. Dijon mustard
2	pounds rainbow trout fillets

Preheat oven to 375°F.

In a food processor, blend first nine ingredients (mayo through Dijon) until smooth. Use immediately or keep in fridge for later use.

Place a sheet of foil over a baking pan and spritz with cooking spray. Lay fillets over foil skin side down.

Spread a dollup of sauce evenly over each fillet. Bake 10 to 15 minutes, depending on the thickness of the fish. Do not over cook the fillets. Plate up immediately with a lemon wedge.

Serves 4.

Tip—We have used dried herbs for this recipe. If available, by all means, use fresh herbs. Try adding or substituting with parsley, chives, thyme or oregano. Use a little more fresh herbs than called for in the recipe.

> Go to your seafood market and try something new. Any of these fish work well with many of our recipes.
>
> arctic char • catfish • flounder • haddock • halibut
> mahi mahi • pollock • rockfish • snapper • tilapia
> turbot • walleye

Trout in Champagne Cream Sauce

Serve this with spinach pasta for a beautiful presentation and enjoy the rest of the champagne with dinner.

Combine champagne, water, allspice, and bay leaf in a wide frying pan. Bring to a boil over high heat. Add trout and reduce heat to low. Cover and simmer until fish is flaky, about 5 to 7 minutes. Cut at the thickest part to test for doneness.

Lift out trout, reserving poaching liquid. Carefully remove skin and any bone and discard. Then break fish into bite sized pieces; set aside.

Strain liquid to remove seasonings and bring to a boil over high heat. Add cream and stir occasionally, reducing sauce to 1¼ cup. Keep warm.

While sauce is cooking, prepare pasta and drain; add sauce to noodles and season with salt and pepper. Add trout and mix lightly with two forks. Serve sprinkled with chives.

Serves 2.

1	cup champagne
2	cups water
½	tsp. whole allspice
1	bay leaf
2	rainbow trout fillets, 7 to 9 oz. each
1¼	cups whipping cream
½	pound dry spinach noodles
2	Tbs. butter
	Salt and pepper
¼	cup chopped chives or sliced green onions with tops

Whole Stuffed Grilled Trout

A true mountain favorite, fresh rainbow trout can be prepared well with little fuss.

2 to 4 whole rainbow trout, gutted and dressed

2 Tbs. olive oil

I lemon, sliced very thin

I red onion, sliced very thin

Sprigs of fresh herbs (One or more of dill, tarragon, chives, rosemary or parsley)

Salt and pepper

Prepare charcoal or gas grill to medium-high heat.

Rinse fish and dry with a paper towel.

Drizzle a little bit of oil inside each fish. Fill each fish with onions, lemon and herbs and season with salt and pepper.

Rub the outside with olive oil and close fish with toothpicks to keep stuffing in.

Grill for 6 to 8 minutes on each side and serve immediately.

Serves 4 to 6, depending on the size of the fish.

Springtime in the mountains is for fishing and foraging. Wild foods are the best. An absolute perfect meal is fresh caught rainbow trout stuffed with ramps along a side of sautéed fiddleheads and morels.

Crab and Shrimp Lasagna

This is a "Figs" creation we serve at the café. It's a New Year's Eve type of dish.

Place a saucepan over medium heat. Sauté onion, garlic, and tarragon in 1 Tbs. butter for one minute. Add shrimp and cook, stirring often until opaque, about 3 minutes. Spoon shrimp mixture into a bowl and set aside.

Melt remaining butter in the saucepan. Add flour and stir until it bubbles. Remove from heat and add cream, broth, and vermouth. Stir constantly over medium heat and bring to a boil. Set aside.

Add any juice from the shrimp to the sauce.

Pour ⅓ of the sauce into a 9×13-inch baking dish. Place a layer of uncooked noodles on top.

Scatter artichoke hearts, spinach and red peppers over noodles. Cover lightly with sauce and cheese.

Add another layer of noodles then half shrimp, crab, and cheese and repeat. Top with remaining sauce.

Bake covered at 350°F for 20 minutes. Uncover and bake 20 to 25 minutes more until golden and bubbly.

Serves 6 to 8.

⅓	cup butter
1	cup thinly sliced green onions
1	clove garlic, minced
½	tsp. dry tarragon
1½	pounds medium shrimp, peeled and deveined
⅓	cup flour
1½	cups whipping cream
1½	cups vegetable or chicken broth
¾	cup dry vermouth or white wine
8	oz. dry lasagna noodles or sheets
1	(16 oz.) can artichoke hearts, drained
1	(10 oz.) pkg. frozen spinach, thawed and squeezed
1	cup roasted red bell peppers, sliced into strips
1	pound crabmeat
2	cups shredded Jarlsberg or Swiss cheese

Dave's Shrimp Risotto

My brother and I collaborated on this recipe. Using short grain brown rice gives this risotto a nice chewy texture. It takes a little longer to cook than white Arborio rice, the traditional risotto grain, so be patient. MBG

7	cups stock
2	Tbs. olive oil
1	cup onion, chopped
2	cloves garlic
1½	cups short grain brown rice
½	cup white wine
1	roasted red pepper, chopped
½	cup parsley
1	pound raw shrimp, peeled (save shells for stock)
1	pound Andouille sausage*, browned
½	cup grated Parmesan cheese

Make stock by following directions on page 33 and add shrimp shells. Keep stock hot.

In a large saucepan, over medium-high heat, sauté onion and garlic in olive oil for about 4 minutes, until beginning to brown.

Add rice, cook one minute. Stir in wine and let soak into rice.

Add stock, ¾ cup at a time, and cook over medium-low heat until liquid is absorbed, stirring occasionally. Continue until rice is tender but firm to the bite.

Slice sausage and brown in a skillet. Remove and drain grease.

Stir in shrimp and red peppers. Remove from heat. Let set one minute then add cooked sausage and Parmesan. Stir gently. Accompany with fresh roasted asparagus or sautéed greens.

Serves 6.

*Andouille is a spicy cajun sausage. Use any type you prefer. Turkey sausage also works well, if you prefer a lighter meat.

Indonesian Grilled Shrimp

Dinner chef Amy Bonfiglio, "Figs", has wooed the White Grass crowd with this fabulous recipe. She serves it with Yellow Rice, (see page 80) and garnishes with chopped cilantro, tomato wedges and sliced lemons.

In a food processor combine onion, garlic, sugar, peanuts, soy sauce, pepper, lemon zest and 5-spice. Blend until almost smooth.

Place shrimp in a glass bowl; pour on onion mixture. Cover and refrigerate 4 to 24 hours.

Grill over hot coals 1 to 2 minutes on each side.

Or cook on the stovetop, in a large skillet over medium heat with a little butter and oil. Lay shrimp, with some of the marinade, evenly in pan. Cook on one side until barely pink. Gently flip and cook 1 to 2 minutes on the other side.

Serves 6.

*If you don't have 5-spice, use ¼ tsp. of each of the following: ground allspice, crushed anise seed, cinnamon, ground cloves and ground ginger.

1	medium onion, cut into chunks
4	cloves garlic
3	Tbs. sugar
2	Tbs. salted roasted peanuts
2	Tbs. soy sauce
1½	tsp. pepper
1	tsp. grated lemon zest
1	tsp. Chinese 5–spice*
1½	pounds large shrimp, peeled and deveined

153

Sea Scallops in Saffron Cream

This luxurious dish goes well with the Greens, Currants and Pine Nuts recipe on page 71.

½ cup dry white wine

½ cup vegetable broth or chicken broth

2 Tbs. shallots or onion, finely minced

1 pinch of saffron

½ cup whipping cream

2 Tbs. butter

1 pound sea scallops, rinsed and drained

In a saucepan, combine wine, broth, shallots or onions, and saffron. Bring to a boil over high heat, uncovered to reduce to about half the volume. Add cream and return to a boil and reduce to about 1 cup of liquid.

Heat a skillet over medium heat. Add 1 Tbs. butter. Cook scallops gently, 1 to 2 minutes on each side (depending on how large scallops are) or until just opaque.

Plate and spoon sauce over scallops. Simply delicious!

Makes 3 to 4 servings.

Saffron is the stigma of a crocus and the most expensive spice in the world. Luckily, it only takes a tiny bit to impart it's warm richness. For best results, let saffron soak in 1 Tbs. water to release it's flavor, then add to the dish.

Steamed Mussels in White Wine

This is a very simple yet delicious meal.
Have some good bread on hand to sop up the broth.

In a large sauté pan with a lid, melt butter over medium heat.

Add onion and garlic. Stir and cook until soft. Add wine, parsley, celery, red pepper, and black pepper.

Bring liquid to a boil and add mussels. Cover with lid and simmer gently until mussels have opened. Do not eat any mussels that are not opened.

Place hot pasta into individual serving bowls and spoon mussels and broth over the top. Garnish with lemon wedges and Parmesan cheese.

Serves 4.

3	Tbs. butter
2	garlic cloves, minced
1/2	cup onion, finely chopped
1	cup dry white wine
1/3	cup fresh parsley, minced
1/4	cup celery, finely chopped
1/4	cup sweet red pepper, finely chopped
	Fresh ground black pepper
2	pounds fresh or frozen mussels
1	pound cooked linguini
	Lemon wedges
	Parmesan cheese

155

Grilled Tuna with Herb Shallot Marinade

Fresh tuna cooked on the grill is delightful. Keep the cooking time to a minimum, medium rare is the most a fresh tuna steak should be cooked.

1/3 cup red wine vinegar
2/3 cup canola oil
1/3 cup shallots, minced
2 cloves garlic, minced
3 Tbs. fresh parsley, minced
2 tsp. dried tarragon
6 fresh tuna steaks

2 sticks butter
1 clove garlic
3 scallions
1/4 tsp. dried basil
1/4 tsp. dried chives
1/8 tsp. tarragon
 Zest of 1/2 lemon
2 tsp. fresh lemon juice
1/4 tsp. black pepper
1 Tbs. fresh parsley

In a small bowl, add vinegar and drizzle in oil, whisking. Add shallots, garlic, parsley and tarragon. Pour over tuna steaks and marinate in a glass dish, refrigerate at least 2 hours.

Prepare grill and place steaks over medium-high heat. Season with salt and pepper.

Grill about 4 minutes on each side.

Top with a teaspoon of lemon herb butter and enjoy.

Serves 6.

Lemon Herb Butter

This seems to make a lot, but it will keep for a month and can be served on any meat, fish, bread or vegetables.

Combine all ingredients in a food processor. Store in the refrigerator.

Bombay Chutney for Fish

This recipe has become one of our all time favorites.
It is has an incredibly fresh and interesting taste. Not to mention, it's easy to make.

Preheat oven to 350°F.

Place all ingredients, except fish in a food processor or blender.

Blend to a smooth consistency.

Place fish fillets skin side down on a lightly oiled sheet pan.

Spread chutney over fish.

Bake uncovered for about 15 to 20 minutes or until fish flakes apart.

Serves 2 to 3 people.

To keep up on what fish is appropriate to eat, check out *www.thefishlist.org*. There you can see what types of fish are safe for your health and for the environment.

3	Tbs. coconut, sweetened or unsweetened
2	Tbs. coconut milk
I	tsp. chili pepper, seeded (serrano or jalapeño)
I	clove garlic, coarsely chopped
I	tsp. fresh ginger root, grated
¼	cup fresh cilantro, chopped
2	Tbs. fresh lime juice
½	tsp. cumin
¼	tsp. salt
I	pound fresh white fish fillets, such as halibut, orange roughy, or tilapia

Sweet Wild Leek (Ramp) Sauce for Fish

This sauce is very thick and more of a spread. It's not just great on any kind of fish — try it on grilled or oven roasted meats.

2	Tbs. olive oil
2	Tbs. butter
1	bunch fresh leeks or about 24 fresh ramps washed and chopped
1	large sweet onion, chopped
6	cloves garlic, minced
1	Tbs. water
1	Tbs. dry white wine
2	tsp. soy sauce
3	tsp. lemon juice
1/4	tsp. black pepper
1	Tbs. balsamic reduction*
1	pound fresh trout fillets
	Lemon wedges for garnish

Heat a large skillet over low heat. Add oil and butter. Then add leeks, onions and garlic. Cook slowly for about 45 minutes, covered, stirring occasionally.

When soft, turn heat up to medium-high, remove lid and cook until onions brown. Stir in water, wine and soy sauce. Remove from heat and stir in salt and pepper. Cool. Transfer to a food processor and blend until smooth. Add lemon juice and balsamic reduction.

Use immediately or store in fridge up to a week. This can also be frozen and used later.

Spread over fish fillets and bake in preheated 375°F oven for 5 to 10 minutes depending on the thickness of the fish. Serve with a lemon wedge.

Serves 2 to 3.

*Balsamic Reduction
In a small skillet, heat 3/4 cup of balsamic vinegar over medium heat. Cook until reduced to a thick syrup — be careful not to let it burn. Vinegar will be sweet and flavorful. Store in a small jar in the fridge for several weeks.

Teriyaki Sauce for Fish

Dinner Chef "Figs" likes to cook with an Asian flair. Use this marinade on salmon, tuna, or your favorite fish. Cooking times will vary, depending on the thickness of the fish.

Preheat oven to 350°F.

Whisk soy sauce, ginger, garlic, sherry, sugar and lemon juice in a bowl.

Line a baking pan with foil and cover with non-stick spray.

Lay fish on foil and spoon marinade onto fish.

Bake uncovered, for 10 to 15 minutes or until fish flakes apart.

Garnish and serve with rice and steamed vegetables for a low fat, delicious meal.

Serves 4.

¼	cup soy sauce
2	tsp. fresh ginger, grated
1	tsp. minced garlic
¼	cup dry sherry
2	tsp. sugar
2	Tbs. lemon juice, fresh
4	fish fillets or steaks, 6 to 8 ounces each
	Lemon wedges, chopped scallions, or chives for garnish

Amy Bonfiglio started at White Grass as a waitress and moved into the chef position shortly thereafter. Her talents include cooking, decorating cakes, rock climbing and trail building. She is currently getting her masters degree in Healing Foods.

Desserts

Chocolate Amaretto Cheesecake

Individual Pumpkin Cheesecakes

Ricotta Cheesecake

Caramel Oatmeal Cake

Betsy's Apple Cake

Chocolate Angel Food Cake

Pumpkin Carrot Cake

Chocolate Zucchini Cupcakes

Texas Sheet Cake

Mini Orange Cupcakes

Chocolate Peppermint Cake

Anise Pizzelles

Chocolate Raspberry Truffle Bars

No Bake Chocolate Almond Cookies

Low Fat Cardamom Cookies

Key Lime Squares

Chocolate Almond Biscotti

Pineapple Chiffon Pie

Peanut Butter Pie

Mom's Pie Crust

Pumpkin Pecan Pie

Blueberry Crisp

Coconut Cream Pie

Apple Galette

Sweet Sauces

Bananas Foster

Canaan Valley Fog

Chocolate Amaretto Cheesecake

Enjoy this reduced fat cheesecake from Pily Henderson.

Preheat oven to 300°F.

Sprinkle chocolate cracker crumbs in bottom of an 8-inch springform pan. Set aside.

Position knife blade in food processor, add cream cheese and next 7 ingredients, processing until smooth.

Add egg and process just until blended. Fold in chocolate chips.

Slowly pour the mixture over the crumbs in pan. Bake for 45 to 50 minutes or until cheesecake is set. Let cool in pan on wire rack.

Cover and chill at least 8 hours. Remove sides of pan and transfer cheesecake to a serving platter. Garnish with chocolate curls, if desired.

Serves 8 to 12.

Chocolate Curls:

Melt ¼ cup chocolate chips over low heat or in microwave. Pour the melted chocolate onto wax paper and spread to a 3-inch wide strip. Let stand until cool but not firm. Pull a vegetable peeler across the chocolate. Transfer the curls to a plate. Store chocolate curls in the freezer.

3	chocolate graham crackers, finely crushed
1½	cups Neufchatel cream cheese
1	cup sugar
1	cup low fat cottage cheese
¼	cup plus 2 Tbs. unsweetened cocoa powder
¼	cup all-purpose flour
¼	cup amaretto liquor
1	tsp. vanilla extract
¼	tsp. salt
1	egg
2	Tbs. semisweet mini chocolate chips
	Chocolate curls (optional garnish)

Individual Pumpkin Cheesecakes

A great make ahead party dessert. Almost too easy for the praise you will receive.

2	(8 oz.) cream cheese (one pound)
½	cup brown sugar
1	(14 oz.) can pumpkin
½	cup sour cream
½	tsp. cinnamon
¼	tsp. ground ginger
⅛	tsp. ground cloves
⅛	tsp. nutmeg
1	tsp. vanilla extract
2	eggs
1	bag ginger snap cookies

Preheat oven to 350°F.

Let cream cheese soften to room temperature. Using a heavy duty mixer, beat cream cheese until smooth. Gradually add sugar, sour cream, then pumpkin. Beat in spices and vanilla. Add eggs, one at a time on low mixer speed.

Use muffin tins and place a paper or foil liner in each, then a single ginger snap in the bottom. Spoon in batter to ¾ full. Bake for about 20 minutes or until cakes are set.

Remove from oven, cool completely. Place in large covered container or zippered plastic bags and store in fridge for up to four days.

Serve topped with whipped cream. Make ahead and freeze for an extra easy dessert.

Makes 20 to 24 cupcakes

For an elegant party dessert platter, serve these with Mini Orange Cupcakes page 172; Key Lime Squares page 178; Chocolate Raspberry Truffle Bars page 175; or Pizzelles page 174.

Ricotta Cheesecake

This is more of a custard than a traditional cheesecake. However, it is a cake and it is made of cheese, so that's what we're calling it.

Preheat oven to 350°F.

Using a mixer, beat ricotta about 2 minutes on medium speed. Then add sugar, vanilla and zest.

Add eggs, one at a time, mixing after each addition.

Pour into a 10-inch spring form pan and bake for 60 to 70 minutes or until cake is set.

Cool and release from pan. Refrigerate and serve with either of the sweet sauces on page 187.

2	pounds (4 cups) ricotta cheese
1	cup sugar
1	tsp. vanilla extract
1	tsp. lemon zest
4	large eggs

Caramel Oatmeal Cake

Always moist, satisfying and tasty, this cake recipe was given to us by Adrienne Sherrill, former café cookie.

1	cup rolled oats
2	cups unbleached white flour
1/4	tsp. salt
1/4	tsp. baking powder
1 1/4	tsp. baking soda
3/4	cup butter, softened (1 1/2 sticks)
1	cup brown sugar
2	eggs
2	tsp. vanilla extract
1 1/2	cups buttermilk

Caramel Frosting:

3/4	cup butter
1 1/2	cups brown sugar
3/4	cup milk
3	cups powdered sugar

Preheat oven to 350°F. Grease and flour two 9-inch cake pans.

Put oats in a blender and blend to the consistency of cornmeal. Combine oats, flour, salt, baking powder and soda in a mixing bowl. Set aside.

In another bowl, cream butter and sugar. Add eggs, one at a time, beating well after each addition. Combine vanilla and buttermilk and add alternately with the flour mixture until well blended.

Pour into prepared pans and bake about 30 minutes or until cake starts to pull away from the sides of the pan. Cool in pans about 5 minutes and turn out onto cooling racks.

Serves 12.

Caramel Frosting:

Heat butter in medium saucepan until melted. Stir in brown sugar. Heat to boiling, stirring constantly. Reduce heat to low. Boil and stir 2 minutes. Stir in milk. Heat to boiling, and then remove from heat. Cool to lukewarm.

Gradually stir in powdered sugar. Place saucepan into bowl of cold water. Beat frosting until smooth and spreadable. If too stiff, add more milk, one teaspoon at a time. Frost cake and enjoy!

Betsy's Apple Cake

This incredibly moist cake recipe was given to us by our dear friend, Betsy Reed. We miss you.

Combine apples and sugar in a large bowl and let stand.

In a small bowl, beat eggs, oil and vanilla. In another bowl, combine flour, soda, cinnamon, and salt.

Alternately add egg mixture and the flour mixture into the apples. Stir in nuts.

Pour into a greased and floured 9×13-inch pan.

Bake at 350°F for about one hour or until an inserted knife comes out clean. Cool cake and frost with the following.

Icing:

4   Tbs. butter
1   cup brown sugar
¼   cup milk

Place all ingredients into a small saucepan and bring to a boil. Remove from heat and spread over cake while icing is still hot. The icing will seep down into the cake. This cake will keep well in the refrigerator for up to one week.

4	cups unpeeled chopped tart cooking apples
2	cups sugar
2	eggs, beaten
½	cup vegetable oil
2	tsp. vanilla extract
2	cups all-purpose flour
2	tsp. baking soda
2	tsp. cinnamon
1	tsp. salt
1	cup chopped walnuts
1	cup raisins (optional)

Chocolate Angel Food Cake

This low fat classic is not difficult to prepare.
Be sure to read and follow directions to create a perfect cake.

2⁄3 cup cake flour

1⁄3 cup cocoa powder

1⁄4 tsp. cinnamon

1⁄4 cup sugar

12 cold egg whites

1 tsp. cream of tartar

2 tsp. water

1 tsp. vanilla

1⁄2 tsp. salt

1 cup sugar

Sift together flour, cocoa, cinnamon and 1⁄4 cup sugar, set aside.

Beat egg whites, cream of tartar, water, vanilla and salt with a heavy duty mixer at medium speed for about 3 minutes until soft–do not beat at a high speed, they should not be stiff.

Gradually add 1 cup sugar, 2 tablespoons at a time at medium speed, for 2 to 3 minutes. You should have a creamy white foam that is soft and glossy.

Transfer egg whites to a large, wide bowl and sift in one quarter of the dry ingredients. Gently fold. Do not stir or mix. Keep folding in until all cocoa and flour are blended well. Pour into a clean, ungreased tube pan, level the top and bake in a preheated 350°F oven for 35 to 40 minutes. Insert a toothpick or wooden skewer; cake is done when it comes out clean.

Remove from oven and invert the cake to cool. Rest it on a rack, or place the tube over a bottle and let the cake stand, upside down until completely cool (at least an hour). Remove by running a thin knife around the edges and along the bottom of the pan.

Serve within 2 days for best results. Serve with sliced strawberries and whipped cream or Apple Raspberry Sauce, page 187.

Serves 6 to 8.

Pumpkin Carrot Cake

An autumn version of our original carrot cake, this very moist cake can be made days ahead of time. It's so good, you may decide to serve it without the icing.

Get two bowls. In one, mix all the dry ingredients and mix wet ingredients in the other. Add the dry to the wet ingredients. Blend well.

Bake in either two greased 10-inch cake pans, three 8-inch cake pans, one 9×13-inch sheet pan or three 1-dozen muffin tins lined with papers.

Bake at 350°F for 30 to 40 minutes. Cool about ten minutes and gently remove from pans. Cool completely and frost, or wrap in plastic wrap and store in fridge until ready to finish.

Cream Cheese Frosting

2   Tbs. butter, softened
1   (8 oz.) cream cheese
2¼ cups powdered sugar
1   tsp. grated orange peel

Soften butter and cream cheese to room temperature. Beat with an electric mixer. Add sugar, vanilla and orange peel, beat until smooth. This will keep, refrigerated, for about a week.

Dry ingredients:

1½ cups whole wheat pastry flour
1   cup all-purpose flour
2   tsp. baking soda
2   tsp. cinnamon
½   tsp. salt
½   tsp. nutmeg
½   tsp. ground ginger
½   tsp. ground cloves

Wet ingredients:

1   cup granulated sugar
¾   cup brown sugar
1   cup buttermilk
½   cup vegetable oil
4   eggs
½   tsp. vanilla
1   (15 oz.) can pumpkin
1   pound grated carrots
1   cup chopped walnuts
1   cup coconut
½   cup raisins

Chocolate Zucchini Cupcakes

This might be the 1,000th thing to do with zucchini, but according to Julie Dzaack , it's one of the best. There's nothing like adding the power of vegetables to your desserts.

2½ cups all-purpose flour
¼ cup cocoa powder
1 tsp. baking soda
½ tsp. salt
½ cup oil
½ cup butter
1¾ cup sugar
2 eggs
1 tsp. vanilla
½ cup buttermilk
2 cups grated zucchini
6 oz. chocolate chips

Preheat oven to 350°F.

Mix flour, cocoa, soda and salt.

In a separate bowl, cream oil, butter and sugar until light and fluffy.

Beat in eggs, one at a time and stir in vanilla. Alternately add dry mixture with buttermilk. Stir in zucchini.

Fill paper lined muffin tins ¾ full and top with chocolate chips. Bake for 20 minutes.

Makes about 2 dozen cupcakes.

Texas Sheet Cake

This is an easy dessert that is moist and delicious. It also works well for a layer cake. I've even made it for a wedding cake. Place wax paper rounds in the cake pans for easy removal. I use four 10-inch pans and double the recipe. LKL

Preheat oven to 350°F.

Mix flour, sugar, and salt in a mixing bowl and set aside.

In a medium saucepan, melt butter and add water and cocoa, stir well while bringing to a boil. Add to the flour and mix.

Add remaining cake ingredients. Stir and pour into a greased 11×17-inch sheet pan.

Bake at 350°F for 15 to 20 minutes. Cool completely before icing.

To prepare icing, melt butter in a medium saucepan. Add cocoa and milk. Bring to a boil, and then add powdered sugar, vanilla and nuts; spread over cake.

Cake:

2	cups all-purpose flour
2	cups sugar
½	tsp. salt
2	sticks butter
1	cup water
4	Tbs. cocoa powder
1	tsp. baking soda
2	eggs, beaten
1	tsp. vanilla
½	cup sour cream

Icing:

1	stick butter (½ cup)
6	Tbs. cocoa powder
6	Tbs. milk
1	pound powdered sugar
1	tsp. vanilla
1	cup pecans or walnuts, chopped (optional)

Mini Orange Cupcakes

This is a special occasion cupcake. An arrangement of these on a large plate makes an elegant addition to a dessert table.

1	cup butter (2 sticks)
1	cup sugar
2	eggs
1	tsp. baking soda
1	tsp. baking powder
½	tsp. salt
3	cups all-purpose flour
¾	cup buttermilk
⅓	cup orange juice
¼	cup chopped golden raisins
1	tsp. vanilla extract
	Zest of 2 oranges (see page 99)

Cream butter and sugar; add eggs and beat well.

Combine dry ingredients in a separate bowl and add alternately to butter mixture with buttermilk and orange juice. Then add raisins, zest and vanilla.

Spoon batter into greased mini muffin tins (tart sized) and bake at 350°F for 15 to 20 minutes. Cool. Dip in syrup recipe below.

Syrup:

Juice of 2 oranges
2 cups sugar
Zest of 2 oranges

In a saucepan, combine orange juice, zest and sugar. Boil until thickened and remove from heat. Dip each cooled cupcake in syrup. Store in airtight container for up to three days or freeze until serving.

Makes about 24.

As a little girl, I remember eating these at my neighbor's Christmas party every year. The downstairs was decorated just for the kids and we had our own special finger foods. It was so festive and special and a cherished memory. MBG

Chocolate Peppermint Cake

This cake is very moist and very easy. It can be made a day ahead and makes 12 to 18 servings—so it's a perfect party cake.

Preheat oven to 350°F.

Mix eggs, sugar, syrup and butter in a mixing bowl. Add flour, salt, powder and vanilla; blend well.

Pour into a 9×13-inch greased baking pan.

Bake for 25 to 30 minutes. While cake is baking, make icing.

Icing:

In a saucepan, heat butter, sugar and milk over medium heat. Bring to a low boil and stir for 2 minutes—don't over cook.

Remove from heat and add chocolate chips, vanilla and mint. Stir until melted. Pour over cake while both are still hot.

*Hint – When measuring flour, spoon it into measuring cup and level off with a straight edge—do not pack cup full.

Cake:

4	eggs
1	cup sugar
1	(16 oz.) can chocolate syrup
1	stick butter, melted
1	cup all-purpose flour*
1½	tsp. baking powder
1	tsp. vanilla extract
½	tsp. salt

Icing:

1	stick butter
1	cup sugar
½	cup milk
1	cup chocolate chips (5 oz.)
1	tsp. vanilla extract
1	tsp. peppermint extract

173

Anise Pizzelles

Pizzelles are pretty, pressed Italian cookies made with a round waffle-type iron. This recipe makes a lot of cookies, but if you're going to make them, make plenty to share for holidays and parties. They also keep very well in a zip lock bag and you can freeze them. My mom, Gerry makes these for Christmas every year. MBG

1	pound butter, softened
2¼	cups sugar
7	eggs
1½	tsp. vanilla
3	Tbs. anise extract
1	Tbs. anise seed
7	cups all-purpose flour
1	tsp. baking powder
½	tsp. baking soda

Cream butter and sugar in a heavy duty mixer or food processor, with a dough blade, until fluffy.

Add eggs, one at a time, beating well. Mix in flavoring and anise seed.

Add half the flour with the baking powder, add to the sugar mixture and blend. Then add remaining flour and soda. Dough becomes very stiff and hard to stir. You will need to abandon the mixer and use your hands. Chill for an hour.

Heat pizzelle iron and roll chilled dough into little balls (about one tablespoon of dough per cookie). Press cookies for 30 to 45 seconds and remove with a fork to a cooling rack. Cool completely before storing.

Makes about 80 cookies.

Chocolate Raspberry Truffle Bars

Here's a delectable choice for any chocolate lover, from Joanne Patterson—hiker, biker, skier, hunter, equestrian, gourmet chef, monumental volunteer and friend.

Preheat oven to 350°F. Grease one 8 or 9-inch square baking pan.

To make brownie layer, melt chocolate chips with butter, mix. Cool slightly. In a large mixing bowl, beat brown sugar and eggs at medium speed until blended. Add chocolate mixture and dissolved coffee and beat well. Stir in flour and baking powder. Spread evenly in a greased 8-inch baking pan. Bake 30 to 35 minutes or until toothpick comes out clean. Cool on wire rack.

To make truffle layer, melt chocolate chips with coffee powder. In a small mixing bowl, beat cream cheese and preserves at medium speed until smooth. At low speed, add chocolate mixture and powdered sugar. Beat until fluffy. Spread over brownie.

To make glaze, melt chocolate chips with shortening in a small saucepan on the stove. Drizzle over truffle layer.

Chill 2 hours. Cut into small squares. Cover and store in the refrigerator.

Jo likes to freeze these and keep them on hand for company.

Makes 16 to 24 little bars.

Brownie Layer

- 1¼ cups semisweet chocolate chips
- ½ cup butter
- ¾ cup packed brown sugar
- 2 eggs
- 1 tsp. instant coffee powder dissolved in 2 Tbs. water (optional)
- ¾ cup all-purpose flour
- ½ tsp. baking powder

Truffle Layer

- 1 cup semisweet chocolate chips
- ¼ tsp. instant coffee powder (optional)
- 1 package (8 oz.) cream cheese, room temp.
- ½ cup seedless red raspberry preserves
- ¼ cup powdered sugar

Glaze

- ¼ cup semisweet chocolate chips
- 1 tsp. solid vegetable shortening

No Bake
Chocolate Almond Cookies

This recipe is not very glamorous, but it is easy to make when you need some cookies fast. It's also great for kids as a beginner recipe. Be sure to assist youngsters with the boiling part.

1¾ cups granulated sugar

½   cup milk

3   Tbs. butter

4   Tbs. unsweetened cocoa powder

½   cup almond butter

3   cups quick cooking oats

In a medium saucepan, combine sugar, milk, butter and cocoa.

Bring to a boil and cook 1½ minutes.

Remove from heat and stir in almond butter and oats.

Drop by tablespoon onto wax paper. Let cool until hardened.

Makes about 2 dozen.

If you don't have almond butter, of course you can use peanut butter.

Low-Fat Cardamom Cookies

We love cardamom and never miss a chance to use it.

Preheat oven to 350°F.

Line a baking sheet with parchment paper or prepare it with a light coating of cooking spray.

In a large bowl, mix together apple butter, oil, egg, vanilla, and brown sugar until smooth. Stir in raisins, cinnamon, and cardamom. Stir in oats. Add flours, baking soda and salt, to the wet mixture and mix until well blended.

Drop the dough by tablespoonful about 3 inches apart onto the baking sheet. Bake for about 15 minutes or until lightly browned. Cool on racks.

Makes 4 dozen.

¾	cup apple butter
2	Tbs. canola oil
1	egg, lightly beaten
2	tsp. vanilla
¾	cup packed brown sugar
¾	cup chopped raisins
1	tsp. cinnamon
1	tsp. ground cardamom
2	cups rolled oats
1	cup unbleached white flour
½	cup whole wheat pastry flour
1	tsp. salt
1	tsp. baking soda

Cardamom is a seed pod from a plant that's in the same family as ginger. It is a fragrant, unique spice that works well in both sweet and savory dishes. The freshest flavor comes from whole green pods. Smash the pods with the flat side of a knife. Remove seeds and crush with a mortar and pestle or use a coffee grinder; add to recipe immediately.

Key Lime Squares

This recipe makes a great addition to a party platter. Cut into 1-inch squares, arrange on a tray and garnish with fresh strawberries or plate alternately with brownie squares.

Crust:

2	sticks butter (1 cup)
2	cups all-purpose flour
½	cup powdered sugar

Filling:

4	eggs beaten
2	cups sugar
½	tsp. salt
6	Tbs. Key lime juice (or lime juice)
1	tsp. baking powder
4	Tbs. flour

Mix all crust ingredients in a bowl and then press into a 9×13-inch sheet pan with edges.

Bake at 350°F for about 10 to 12 minutes or until lightly browned. Cool crust while preparing and making the filling.

Whisk together all ingredients in a bowl and pour over crust. Bake for about 15 to 20 minutes or until liquid is set. Cool slightly and dust the top with powdered sugar before cutting.

Makes 12 large or 20 small squares.

Chocolate Almond Biscotti

This is a variation of the biscotti recipe from our first book, "Cross Country Cooking".

In a large bowl, combine almonds, flour, sugar, salt, baking powder, cocoa, and chocolate chips.

In a separate bowl, lightly whisk eggs and extracts. Add the egg mixture to the dry mixture and mix well. Lightly knead the dough in the bowl with your hands until it all holds together.

Divide the dough into 3 equal parts and roll each into a log about 2 inches wide.

Place each log 4 inches apart on a large greased baking sheet. Bake at 350°F for 45 minutes. Remove from oven and cool for 10 minutes. Slice logs into ½-inch pieces.

Reduce oven to 300°F and return sliced cookies to baking sheet. Bake for 10 to 15 minutes more. Cool completely and store in an airtight container.

Makes 3 dozen cookies.

Biscotti (which means "twice baked") are supposed to be hard and dry. They are excellent for dunking in coffee, tea, hot chocolate or milk.

½ cup almonds, sliced and toasted
2¾ cups all-purpose flour
1 cup sugar
½ tsp. salt
1 tsp. baking powder
⅓ cup cocoa powder
1 cup mini chocolate chips
3 eggs plus 3 egg yolks
1 tsp. vanilla extract
1 tsp. almond extract

Pineapple Chiffon Pie

A perfect summer dessert; this recipe makes two pies.
They are so light, fluffy and delicious they will go fast.

2 (9-inch) pie crusts, baked and cooled

1 large (16 oz.) and 1 small (4 oz.) can crushed pineapple

2 pkg. plain gelatin

1 cup sugar

3 Tbs. cornstarch

4 eggs, separated

½ tsp. salt

2½ cups buttermilk

Juice and zest of 2 lemons (see page 99)

Bake and cool pie crusts. Use either a homemade (see page 182) or a store bought crust.

Drain pineapple and reserve juice. Dissolve gelatin in ½ cup juice. Set aside.

In a saucepan, over low heat, combine ½ cup sugar, cornstarch, egg yolks, salt and ½ cup buttermilk. Stir constantly until thick, then add 2 cups buttermilk, remove from heat and cool.

Then add softened gelatin, 3 Tbs. lemon juice and grated zest. Chill filling at least 30 minutes then fold in 1½ cups pineapple.

Whip egg whites until soft mounds appear. Gradually add ½ cup sugar and whip until stiff peaks form. Gently fold whites into pineapple mixture. Spoon into cooled pie shells. Refrigerate until serving.

This is what my father and I requested as our birthday cakes every year. Of course, it was made with homemade crust. My mom makes the best pie crust. Everyone says that, don't they? MBG

Peanut Butter Pie

After a day of skiing, there is less guilt when indulging in desserts. So ski and eat up.

Combine graham crackers, butter and sugar and press into a 10-inch pie plate. Place in the refrigerator while preparing the filling.

Beat cream cheese, peanut butter, sugar, and vanilla with a mixer on medium speed until smooth.

In a separate bowl, beat cream until it forms stiff peaks. Gently fold the whipped cream into the peanut butter mixture and spread into the pie shell. Cover with plastic wrap and refrigerate until firm (about 4 hours).

Topping:

For the topping, bring cream and butter to boil in a small saucepan. Lower the heat and add chocolate chips to the pan. Stir to dissolve the chips. Cool topping to lukewarm. Remove plastic wrap from pie and spread topping on with a knife. Garnish with peanuts.

Refrigerate for 1 hour or until ready to serve.

Serves 6 to 8.

---

1 1/2 cups graham cracker crumbs, plain or chocolate, crushed

6 Tbs. melted butter

1/4 cup sugar

1 (8oz.) cream cheese, softened

1 cup peanut butter, chunky or smooth

1/2 cup sugar

2 tsp. vanilla

1 cup heavy cream, cold

Topping:

2 Tbs. butter

1/3 cup heavy cream

1/4 cup chocolate chips

1/4 cup peanuts, chopped

Mom's Pie Crust

My mom uses all shortening, but I use half butter and shortening. Some say that lard makes a good crust. You will have to work with it and see which you like best. This recipe may seem overwhelming, but you can get hooked on making pie crust from scratch, I did. MBG

1	cup all-purpose flour
1/2	tsp. salt
1/2	tsp. sugar
2 1/2	Tbs. vegetable shortening (like Crisco)
2 1/2	Tbs. butter, cold
3	to 4 Tbs. ice water

Place flour, salt and sugar in a bowl. Add shortening, blend with a pastry cutter, or by cutting in opposite directions with two knives. Then blend in butter until you have coarse crumbs with some pea-sized pieces. Or you can use a food processor to mix the dough. Pulse gently for 1 second at a time, don't over mix.

In the bowl, sprinkle one tablespoon of water over different parts of mixture. Toss quickly with a fork until particles stick together when pressed gently. Use only enough water to make the particles cling together. Dough should not be wet or slippery. Form into two equal balls. Wrap in plastic wrap and refrigerate at least 30 minutes and up to 24 hours. Dough can be frozen for later use.

Remove dough from fridge, let set 5 minutes. To roll out dough, scatter a little flour and sugar over your work surface. Flour the rolling pin as well. Flatten dough ball and gently begin to roll out from center to all directions. Turn dough as needed and sprinkle more flour and sugar as needed. You may have to "cut and paste" areas to make a round shape. Roll to about 1/8-inch thick.

Fold circle in half, gently, then quartered. Pick up and lay in pie pan. Then unfold, gently. Trim, leaving 3/4″ overhanging. Tuck that under and pinch around the rim for an edge.

To bake an empty crust, first refrigerate about 30 minutes. Cover the shell with foil and line it with 1/2 cup dried beans. This will keep it from puffing up. Bake in preheated 400°F oven for 20 minutes. Then gently remove foil and beans. Bake an additional 5 to 10 minutes, or until golden brown. Remove from oven and cool.

This recipe makes one 9-inch pie crust.

Pumpkin Pecan Pie

You can mix this pie up pretty quickly. If you use a refrigerated crust, it will be even easier. Just once, try making a crust from scratch, see page 182.

In a large mixing bowl, combine eggs, sugars, pumpkin, milk, flavoring, and pecans. Stir and pour into pie shell. Bake at 350°F for 45 minutes or until pie is set.

1	(9-inch) deep dish pie crust
3	eggs, beaten
¾	cup sugar
½	cup brown sugar
1	cup pumpkin, fresh or canned
1	cup evaporated milk
1	Tbs. rum or bourbon
1	cup pecan halves

Blueberry Crisp

If blueberries aren't available, use raspberries, blackberries, apples, peaches—or a combination. You can't go wrong. We take advantage of the wild blueberries that grow here in the mountains. One could make a full time job of berry picking in the summer - the bears can't eat them all.

3	cups blueberries, fresh or frozen
¾	cup butter, room temperature
¾	cup all-purpose flour
¾	cup brown sugar
¾	cup rolled oats

Pour blueberries into a 9-inch pie pan.

In a bowl, mix remaining ingredients well, using your hands.

Evenly scatter topping over berries.

Bake at 350°F in a preheated oven for 45 to 50 minutes until top is golden brown.

Serve warm with fresh cream or ice cream.

Eat more blueberries.

They have been ranked the #1 antioxidant among fruits and vegetables. Antioxidants are a defense against cancer, heart disease and the effects of aging. But don't let that be your only reason—blueberries also taste fabulous.

Coconut Cream Pie

This delicious classic dessert was given to us by baker extraordinaire Bobbie Moore, it's actually her mom's recipe. When testing this recipe, Bobbie and I made too much filling. We later served it over fresh sliced peaches. Delish! MBG

Cook sugar, cornstarch, salt and milk in a medium-sized heavy saucepan. Cooking over medium heat, slowly add beaten egg yolks. (Keep whites aside for meringue.) Stir constantly and bring to a bare simmer. Remove from heat and whisk until smooth. Return to heat and bring to a simmer again, whisking for 1 minute. Remove from heat and whisk in butter, vanilla and coconut.

Spoon the hot filling into pie crust.

To make meringue, beat room temperature egg whites on medium speed until soft peaks form. Add cream of tartar and gradually add sugar, beating on high until glossy stiff peaks form. Beat in vanilla. Immediately spread over hot pie filling, spreading it all the way to the crust.

Bake in preheated 325°F oven for 20 minutes. Cool and serve or refrigerate.

Makes 1 pie.

You do not have to top this pie with meringue. Simply refrigerate before serving.

Use store bought crust or try making it yourself, see page 182 for instructions.

¾	cup sugar
3	Tbs. cornstarch
¼	tsp. salt
2	cups milk
4	large eggs, separated
2	Tbs. butter
1	tsp. vanilla
1	cup sweetened flaked coconut, toasted, (see page 18)
1	prepared 9-inch pie crust, baked and cooled
¼	tsp. cream of tartar
½	cup sugar
½	tsp. vanilla

Apple Galette

When apple season arrives, this is the dessert to make. Once the crust is made (or bought) it is an easy fix. This rustic, yet elegant tart can be made with pears, peaches or other fruit as well.

1	(9-inch) pie crust
2	to 3 tart cooking apples
1	Tbs. lemon juice
1/8	tsp. ground cinnamon
1/4	cup brown sugar
3	Tbs. flour
	Pinch of nutmeg
1/4	cup granulated sugar

Make a single pie crust (see page 182) and roll into an 11-inch round; or remove prepared dough from fridge.

Peel, core and thinly slice apples. Toss with lemon juice, cinnamon and brown sugar. Then add flour, toss.

Carefully drape dough across a large baking sheet.

Spread fruit over the dough, leaving 3 inches around the sides. Sprinkle with nutmeg.

Fold edges of the dough toward the center and press to seal, leaving fruit exposed at the center.

Bake in preheated 400°F oven for 15 minutes. Reduce heat to 350°F and bake 30 more minutes. Remove from oven when browned and cool on a wire rack.

Make caramel by heating granulated sugar in a saucepan over medium heat, stirring occasionally. Cook about 5 minutes until golden in color. Remove from heat and drizzle over galette.

Serves 6.

Sweet Sauces

Use any of these sweet sauces on any of your favorite desserts.

Lemon Cardamom Sauce

Mix sugar, cornstarch, salt and cardamom in a small saucepan. Gradually add boiling water. Cook over low heat until thick. Stir in butter and lemon juice and zest. Blend thoroughly. Cool. Store in fridge up to a week.

½	cup sugar
1	Tbs. cornstarch
	Pinch of salt
⅛	tsp. ground cardamom
1	cup boiling water
2	Tbs. butter
1	Tbs. fresh lemon juice
	Zest of ½ a lemon

Blueberry Compote

In a saucepan, cook all ingredients over medium heat, stirring until berries cook down to a smooth sauce (about 20 minutes). To make a thicker sauce, mix 1 Tbs. water with 1½ tsp. cornstarch and add to fruit mixture as it cooks. Store in refrigerator for up to five days. Warm before serving if desired.

1	pint fresh or frozen blueberries
¼	cup sugar
1	Tbs. lemon juice
2	Tbs. water

Apple Raspberry Sauce

Place all ingredients in a saucepan, adding only 1 tsp. of sugar at first, you can add more if fruit is too tart. Cook, covered for about 20 minutes, over medium heat until you have a thick sauce. Use immediately or store in fridge.

½	Tbs. butter
3	cups tart apples, chopped and peeled
1	cup raspberries, fresh or frozen
1	ripe peach, diced
1–3 tsp. brown sugar	

Bananas Foster

If you're looking for a last minute, very quick, yet elegant dessert, here it is.
This recipe originated in New Orleans; we make it a little less sweet.
For breakfast, eliminate the rum and serve with pancakes or waffles.

4   ripe bananas, peeled
2   Tbs. butter
2   Tbs. brown sugar
¼   cup rum
     Vanilla ice cream

Heat a large skillet over medium heat, add butter. When melted, add sugar and mix well with a wooden spatula.

Slice bananas in half lengthwise and place in the skillet cut side down. Cook about 3 minutes on each side.

Remove bananas and add rum to skillet. Stir well.

Pour syrup over bananas and serve with vanilla ice cream.

Serves 4.

Canaan Valley Fog

The fog in Canaan Valley is as thick as this delicious dessert drink.

Mix all ingredients in a punch bowl and serve immediately. Serves 12.

2 cups coffee liquor

1/4 cup vodka

5 cups strong black coffee, cold

3 pints soft coffee ice cream

Index

Index

Index

Index

Order More Cookbooks

WHITE GRASS FLAVOR $19.95 + $4.00 shipping and handling = **$23.95**

CROSS COUNTRY COOKING—Our First Cookbook—Published in 1996.
Great cookbook for beginners and seasoned cooks alike.
                                                $13.95 + $3.00 shipping and handling = **$16.95**

Good deal!! Buy **BOTH COOKBOOKS**: including shipping & handling = **$35.00**

WHITE GRASS CAFÉ Logo Apron (has pockets)
(Forest Green with white vegetables and "White Grass Café" screen printed on front)

$18.00 + $3.00 shipping and handling = **$21.00**

White Grass Café
HC 70 Box 299
Freeland Road
Davis, WV 26260

www.whitegrass.com/cafe.html
Email us at: **chip@whitegrass.com**
304-866-4114

White Grass Order Form
Send check or credit card number.

Number of copies _____

Number of aprons _____

_____

Name _____

Address _____

City/State/Zip _____

Phone _____

Credit Card Number _____

Exp. Date _____

Signature _____

West Virginia Culinary Scholarship

In White Grass Café's belief that good tasting, nutritious, high quality food should be the standard, we have formed the West Virginia Culinary Scholarship.

A portion of the proceeds from this book will go into a scholarship fund created by White Grass Café. Every other year the Café will donate $500.00 to a deserving culinary arts student from West Virginia to help them achieve their goal in promoting culinary excellence.

Please contact Laurie Little at 304-866-4114 or go to our website at www.whitegrass.com/cafe.html for more information.

We really hope you enjoy the recipes in this book.

Thanks for your support.

Bon Appétit.

Laurie and Mary Beth